NEW FRENCH PLAYS

Portrait of a Woman by Michel Vinaver, *Struggle of the Dogs and the Black* by Bernard-Marie Koltès, *These Childish Things* by Raymond Cousse, *Stranger in the House* by Richard Demarcy.

David Bradby is Professor of Drama and Theatre Studies at London University. He has taught at the Universities of Glasgow, Kent, Ibadan and Caen. His publications include *People's Theatre* (Croom Helm, 1978), *Modern French Drama 1940–1980* (Cambridge University Press, 1984); *Directors' Theatre* (Macmillan 1988). He has directed many plays by modern French dramatists including Sartre, Beckett, Adamov and Vinaver.

Claude Schumacher is senior lecturer in Theatre Studies at Glasgow University. He is the editor of *Theatre Research International* and has written *Jarry and Apollinaire* (Macmillan, 1985) and edited Marivaux: Plays (Methuen, 1988).

NEW FRENCH PLAYS

PORTRAIT OF A WOMAN
by
Michel Vinaver

STRUGGLE OF THE DOGS AND THE BLACK
by
Bernard-Marie Koltès

THESE CHILDISH THINGS
by
Raymond Cousse

STRANGER IN THE HOUSE
by
Richard Demarcy

Selected and introduced by
David Bradby and Claude Schumacher

Methuen Drama

A METHUEN PAPERBACK

First published in Great Britain as a Methuen paperback original in 1989 by Methuen Drama, Michelin House, 81 Fulham Road, London SW3 6RB. Distributed in the USA by HEB Inc. 70 Court Street, Portsmouth, New Hampshire 03801

Selection and introduction copyright © 1989 David Bradby and Claude Schumacher

Portrait d'une femme (*Portrait of a Woman*) © 1989 by Michel Vinaver and Donald Watson
Combat de nègre et de chiens (*Struggle of the Dogs and the Black*) © 1989 by Bernard-Marie Koltès and Matthew Ward
Enfantillages (*These Childish Things*) © 1989 by Raymond Cousse and Brian Singleton
L'Étranger dans la maison (*Stranger in the House*) © 1989 by Richard Demarcy and Helen Garner

British Library Cataloguing in Publication Data

New French Plays by Cousse, Demarcy, Koltès and Vinaver
  1. Drama in French, 1945–
  Anthologies–English texts
  1. Cousse, Raymond, 1942.
  II Schumacher, Claude
  842'. 914 '08

  ISBN 0-413-19400-0

Printed and bound in Great Britain by Richard Clay Ltd, Bungay, Suffolk

CAUTION
All rights whatsoever in these plays are strictly reserved and applications for performance, readings etc, must be made before rehearsals to Methuen Drama, Michelin House, 81 Fulham Road, London SW3 6RB.

CONTENTS

INTRODUCTION

The report published in 1987 by the *Centre National des Lettres* lists 106 contemporary French playwrights whose work is regularly performed by professional companies.[1] This list is not exhaustive: the 1980s has been a strikingly productive period for French dramatists. The generous cultural policies of the French government since the first election of François Mitterrand in 1981 have encouraged an expansion of dramatic activity. Global subsidies to the theatre in France today stand at around £100 million. Spending on such a scale means that no medium-sized town in France is without its professional theatre company; moreover the increased Arts spending masterminded in the early 1980s by Jack Lang, Mitterrand's Minister of Culture, was arranged so as to favour the production of new writing. On the publishing side, things are not so rosy, (although there is some improvement in this sector, too). Despite the large quantity of new work being performed, the French book-buying public (unlike its British counterpart) seems to have lost the habit of reading plays. Hence the enquiry instituted by the *Centre National des Lettres* to try and find out why more plays were not being published.

The detailed conclusions of this enquiry can be summed up simply: in recent years those involved in producing theatre have conducted a vigorous campaign for the recognition of drama as an art form independent of general literature, and they have been almost too successful for their own good. In earlier periods the theatre was an important outlet for writers who also published in other genres. Claudel, Cocteau, Gide, Sartre, Camus are all examples of authors whose dramatic writing was only a part of their activity as poets, thinkers, novelists, *hommes de lettres*. Some of them were closely involved in the practical work of theatre companies but they did not feel that their plays were exclusively destined for performance: they should also be able to stand as autonomous works fit for private reading. Sartre even went so far as to say that although he enjoyed the excitement of a first night, what really counted for him was the published book.

The cultural impact of 1968 helped change this view. The near revolution of that year caught most theatre companies by surprise. They had not foreseen it and were therefore unable to contribute. This was felt to be a serious failure by many working in the regional theatres. The majority had been drawn into theatre work inspired by the ideals of the *théâtre populaire* movement. They held an evangelistic belief in the civic responsibility of theatre to reflect the life of the community and to provide a space in which to debate the profound concerns of that community. They believed it was especially important for such theatres to address themselves to the broad mass of the population, employing terms that they could understand, and involving them in active participation. The theatre of the 1960s had sustained and built up these expectations. André Malraux, Minister of Culture under de Gaulle, had presided over a massive expansion of theatre provision in the French regions. Brecht's plays had been translated and widely performed and this had opened the way to writers such as Armand Gatti, Aimé Césaire, Gabriel Cousin, in whose work dramaturgical experiment went hand in hand with revolutionary politics. But despite the growth of such work, Molière and Shakespeare continued to be by far the most frequently performed authors, and many theatre workers concluded that an excessive emphasis on the classics had led them to lose touch with the preoccupations of the people.

Their solution, however, was not to turn to contemporary playwrights. Instead they decided that, since no existing work could meet the needs of the moment, it was up to those actively involved in theatre work to supply the remedy by devising new material and by performing it in places and at times acceptable to the mass audience. At this point a second demand came into play: for more democratic practices within the theatre companies themselves. The 1960s had seen a considerable extension of the power of the director. At this time directors were the direct recipient of the Government theatre subsidy: it was up to them to make the decisions regarding repertoire, policy, staffing, etc. Together with the demand for a theatre of broad popular appeal went the insistence that every member of the company should have a share in decision making. The slogan of the day was the right for everyone to participate in the creative process – *la création collective*. For several years in the early 1970s a large number of the more prominent theatre companies put on only collectively devised shows. The most successful were those which, like Ariane Mnouchkine's Théâtre du Soleil, were also experimenting with new forms of playing space and actor-audience relationship. *1789*, by the Théâtre du Soleil, was designed for performance on a basketball pitch on the assumption that this was a common public space available almost anywhere in France. This novel space provoked a new relationship with the audience: no longer seated in passive rows lined up in front of the action, they were constantly on the move, sometimes surrounded by action on all sides, sometimes grouped around a central event.

This preoccupation with forms of group work was enhanced by foreign influences. Partly thanks to the extraordinarily successful Nancy Festival of New Theatre run by Jack Lang, French audiences had their first glimpse of new work by the Bread and Puppet theatre, Grotowski's Laboratory Theatre, Bob Wilson's *Deafman Glance*, the Teatro Campesino – all companies which elaborated their own scenic material with little or no dependence on the work of a playwright. The way to establish a specific language of theatre seemed to be by abandoning words in favour of images. These were exciting times for everyone involved in theatre work with one exception: the playwright. His services no longer appeared necessary. When texts were used as the basis for performance, they were often non-dramatic texts as in Antoine Vitez's *Cathérine*, a version of Aragon's novel *Les Cloches de Bâle* or the Théâtre du Campagnol's adaptation of *David Copperfield*. If a writer *were* lucky enough to find employment, he had to put up with seeing his texts rewritten by committee. Carried away by the new theatre of images, the public no longer wanted to buy plays to read. Publishers with theatre lists closed them down; professional writers no longer saw the stage as a natural outlet for their work. In Britain the relatively large output of television drama creates a regular demand for playwrights and for dramatic work from authors not principally working in the theatre. In France the demand is much less and it seemed for a while as though 'the playwright' were doomed to extinction.

The sharp improvement that has taken place over the last decade can be attributed to many factors. One of the most important is the willingness of the large subsidised theatre companies to appoint *dramaturges* on the German model: i.e. writers whose job is to prepare translations and adaptations, but also to produce original dramatic work. Michel Deutsch at Strasbourg and Daniel Besnehard at Caen are outstanding examples; many others could be cited. The practice of employing a *dramaturge* became more common as a growing awareness of the difficulties of *création collective* developed. Even the companies that achieved major successes found that the strain of this way of working tore them apart after a few seasons. When additional funds were made available to increase theatre production the need for the playwright was bound to be felt once more. The new generation of dramatic writers have not all worked as *dramaturges*; many are people who had previously worked in theatre as actors or directors. Outstanding examples of directors who are also playwrights are Roger Planchon, director of the Théâtre National Populaire at Villeurbanne (Lyon) and Gildas Bourdet, director of the Théâtre National de la Salamandre at Lille. Among the many actors who have also developed careers as playwrights are two of the most commercially successful: Jean-Claude Grumberg and Loleh Bellon. Both have had plays translated into English and performed in London. (It is worth noting that the most admired English playwrights in France are Harold Pinter, who also began as an actor, and James Saunders; the work of Griffiths, Hare, Brenton, Churchill, Edgar or Bond has so far made little significant impact.)

In addition to the stimulus provided from within the theatre profession, there has been a significant effort since 1981 to increase the number of plays published in France. Through the *Centre National des Lettres* money has been made available to pay for up to 50% of production costs and two new play collections have appeared: *Théâtrales* published by EDILIG and *Papiers* published by Actes Sud. Further stimulus is provided by Théâtre Ouvert, run by the broadcaster Lucien Attoun, an organisation whose sole purpose is to promote new writing for the theatre. Théâtre

Ouvert runs a series of *tapuscrits* – typescripts of plays that are circulated around the professional theatre circuit – and also publishes a few plays for commercial sale. It has a small workshop theatre in Pigalle where it stages readings and productions of new work and also offers writers the chance of working with actors on unfinished plays or on sections of plays that they wish to 'test' in performance.

In all these different ways French playwrights have become increasingly involved in the active process of theatre work. This also helps to explain why theatre sometimes seems to have become a specialised field no longer open to any professional writer. Each of the four writers whose work is published in this volume has close connections with a director or theatre company: Patrice Chéreau chose the play by Koltès as the opening production of his Théâtre des Amandiers in 1984 and has directed all Koltès's subsequent work; Richard Demarcy has his own theatre company – the Naïf Théâtre – with over a dozen original productions to its credit; Michel Vinaver has worked with many of France's major directors: Roger Planchon, Jean-Marie Serreau, Antoine Vitez, Jacques Lassalle and for the past decade he has collaborated with Alain Françon, director of the Théâtre Eclaté of Annecy. Raymond Cousse is a whole theatre company in himself, having performed his work regularly at the *Lucernaire* theatre complex in Montparnasse run by Christian Le Guillochet.

Despite the volume and intensity of dramatic activity, it is difficult to identify a single dominant tendency or style in French theatre today. The genre that has suffered most in recent years is the 'boulevard play', that peculiarly Parisian mixture of sex and wit that provided the capital's commercial theatres with their staple diet for the first half of this century. The main function of such plays was always to show off the talents of a couple of star actors and this role has been taken over by the cinema. The French film industry turns out a large quantity of mediocre films simply as a vehicle for audience-pulling stars like Philippe Noiret or Claude Brasseur, Fanny Ardent or Isabelle Adjani. Whereas the West End theatres of London have remained commercially strong by adapting to new kinds of plays and welcoming in the successors of the 'Angry Young Men', the privately owned theatres of Paris have been very unresponsive to change and have experienced a steady decline. Relatively few authors have appeared to continue the tradition of Marcel Achard or André Roussin and there is no obvious successor to Jean Anouilh, the last of a line of playwrights whose work appealed to the intellectual community as well as to the boulevard public, and whose heyday was in the inter-war years with Stève Passeur, Edouard Bourdet, Charles Vildrac, Henri-René Lenormand, Bernard Zimmer and Alexandre Arnoux.

The English-speaking theatre has been dominated for so long by the heritage of naturalism, that it comes as something of a shock to find continental playwrights turning from grotesque or poetic theatre to explore once again the possibilities offered by naturalist form. This is a strong current in French playwriting today, often occurring in conjunction with war-time subject matter as in Daniel Besnehard's plays about Normandy during the Occupation or Jean-Claude Grumberg's *The Workshop* (*L'Atelier*) depicting the sweatshops of the clothing industry in the 1940s. There are frequent autobiographical elements in these plays, as if only now can the pain of living through those years be explored. It is striking that the French still seem preoccupied with the horrors of the Second World War to the exclusion of the more recent conflict in Algeria in the 1950s: no significant play has yet been written about the Algerian war with the exception of Genet's *The Screens (Les Paravents)* and the plays of the Algerian poet Kateb Yacine.

Other writers, who choose to set their work in contemporary France, develop apparently naturalistic situations to the point where they tip over into 'hyperrealism'. This term is used to describe an absolute faithfulness to detail so that the situation depicted takes on an hallucinatory quality. This was the case with Gildas Bourdet's play *Station Service* in 1986 in which, as well as the hyperrealistic depiction on stage of a service station, there was also a determination to achieve total faithfulness to language as spoken in real life. This was so successful that parts of the play were almost incomprehensible to anyone not familiar with the idioms of North-East France, where the play was set.

This combination of naturalistic detail in stage setting and close observation of linguistic detail is also characteristic of another current in French playwriting, known as *théâtre du quotidien*. This is the name given to a number of playwrights whose work was influenced by contemporary German-speaking authors and film makers, especially Handke, Kroetz, Fassbinder, Sperr, Achternbusch. These writers confront their audiences with fragmentary scenes showing ordinary, often inarticulate people in situations that are also very ordinary, but presented in a style of heightened realism. From behind this ordinariness there emerges the hidden violence of contemporary social structures and through these inarticulate people we are shown how language can control and form character. Authors commonly classed in this school of *théâtre du quotidien* include Jean-Paul Wenzel, René Kalisky, Bernard Chartreux and Michel Deutsch, all of whom came to prominence in the 1970s. They have been followed, in the last decade, by a new generation of writers with similar preoccupations, though they form less of a 'school', including Enzo Cormann, Daniel Besnehard, Denise Bonal, Louise Doutreligne, Daniel Lemahieu. Set in recognisable, everyday situations the plays of the *quotidien* playwrights are peopled by characters who are overwhelmed by language, language that they struggle to make their own, but are unable to dominate: it ends up by invading every aspect of their being, with the result that they are destroyed by vain attempts to give it shape and integrity.

VINAVER

Michel Vinaver (born 1927) is the outstanding dramatist of the *théâtre du quotidien*. His plays enact the crisis between human beings and their language, as do those of Deutsch, Wenzel, etc., but his scope is much broader, encompassing the worlds of business and commerce. He is the only performed playwright in contemporary France who is seeking to dramatize the realities of industry and marketing under late twentieth-century capitalism. This is in sharp contrast to Britain, where plays like Caryl Churchill's recent success *Serious Money* are less unusual. Vinaver began his literary career as a novelist, with two works published in quick succession: *Lataume* (1950) and *L'Objecteur* (1951). His first play, written in 1955, was entitled *Aujourd'hui ou les Coréens (Today or the Koreans)*; like the two novels, it revealed a strong preoccupation with everyday experience that owed something to the existentialist thought of Albert Camus. Vinaver had met Camus when he was still a student and developed a great admiration for his work. But he did not imitate Camus's use of myth or historical distance when he began to write plays, preferring to stick as closely as possible to the experience of contemporary reality. The action of his first play alternates between half a dozen French soldiers in the Korean war who have lost contact with their regiment and a group of Korean villagers. One of the soldiers stumbles on the village, where he is accepted and becomes integrated into the life of the community. In this process the fixed ideologies and stereotypes that have hitherto structured his perception of life simply fall away and lose their use. The play manages to present the reality of human contact in the here and now as a fundamentally political experience despite, or perhaps because of, the way it slips between the categories of received political discourse.

The majority of Vinaver's twelve published plays deal with people in working situations, for example *Les Travaux et les jours*, 1978 (performed at the Orange Tree, Richmond in 1987 as *A Smile at the end of the line*), which is set in the after-sales office of a firm manufacturing coffee grinders; *Par-dessus bord*, (*Overboard*), 1969 which tells the story of an old-fashioned French toilet-paper manufacturer facing up to the challenge of American-imported 'softies'. In this respect, his most recent play, *Portrait of a Woman*, is an exception: it is the only one to be set in a period other than the present. The play is, however, closely based on accounts of the real case of Pauline Dubuisson, a medical student who murdered her lover and was condemned to hard labour for life in 1951. Vinaver followed the case at the time, collecting the daily accounts of the trial that were published in *Le Monde*. Having put the cuttings away in an attic (along with the steadily accumulating mass of such documents that he keeps), Vinaver forgot all about it until the early 1980s, when he rediscovered the file. On re-reading it, he was struck by the way in which the court authorities failed to persuade Pauline Dubuisson to enter into their linguistic field. She adopted none of the attitudes expected in such circumstances: she was neither contrite nor angry – she simply appeared untouched by the court's proceedings. Vinaver decided to construct a play based not so much on the murder as on the accounts of the trial and he chose to limit himself to those published in *Le Monde*: every word that was reported as having been spoken in court would be included in the play.

The result is a fragmentary dialogue comprising a multiplicity of voices. The various witnesses speak a bewildering variety of different idioms, whose ideological presuppositions are gradually revealed through their words and their manner of speaking them. But the central character (renamed Sophie Auzanneau) seems untouched by the confrontations in the courtroom; her replies simply do not coincide with the expectations of her questioners. Her own emotional needs only emerge from the flash-back scenes evoking her relationships with parents, friends, lovers, teachers. But here, too, she is in conflict with other people's expectations of her: each of these people has a particular idea of what she should be, an image that each tries to impose upon her. When her behaviour or her language fail to coincide with what her interlocutors expect of her they make no attempt to adapt or adjust (with the exception of Xavier) and we gradually see how each of these relationships is, to some degree, a power relationship: Sophie is never allowed to take a dominant role. If she had been able to impose her view of herself and of social relations on the others, or if she had been able to integrate the different 'selves' that she manifests in her different relationships, then she might have been able to survive. As it is, she can only experience life as a sum of fragmented parts with no centre to hold it together. Her crime is an act of desperation, a protest against the intolerable strain of trying to pull together so many separate, subservient selves. It is clear that her predicament is to a large extent the consequence of having to conform to role models proposed by men. Her lover, her teacher, her father, her boyfriend, all in different ways, cast her in roles that condemn her to passivity, denying her the possibility of personal development or fulfilment. Her one real ally is the landlady, Mme Guibot, whose sympathy is not enough to make up for her inability to understand Sophie.

There are obvious similarities between Sophie and Camus's Meursault in *L'Étranger (The Outsider)*: both are victims of a legal process that functions according to its own logic, taking little account of the real needs of the character concerned. But Sophie is never able to achieve the positive affirmation of Meursault, who despite being crushed by the pressures of social conformism, is able, before he dies, to affirm his rightness and declare his revolt. This is denied to Sophie, since Vinaver had decided to remain faithful to his source. It would have been easy to write a final speech in which she vindicates herself, but it would have falsified the truth of her dilemma, painstakingly recreated for the audience in the course of the play. The independent life-style enjoyed by Meursault (before his crime) was not available to a woman in Sophie's circumstances, growing up in the France of the late 1940s. Sophie Auzanneau is a martyr deprived of a voice, looking forward to the changed world of the 1980s, in which women may find an independent voice and in which theatre can be used to express it. There is a tragic afterword to this case: in 1964 the real Pauline Dubuisson was released from prison with a remission of sentence for exemplary behaviour. A year and a half later she committed suicide.

Vinaver's recent work has been very well received in France. The première of *Les Voisins (Neighbours)* in 1986 won the Kleist prize for the best production of the year and, coinciding with this production, Vinaver's complete plays were published in two volumes by Actes Sud in collaboration with L'Aire of Lausanne. The production of *Les Voisins* opened at Théâtre Ouvert's small theatre in Paris and then went on an extended tour of regional theatres, receiving glowing reviews and earning Vinaver the (slightly misleading) title of 'the French Chekhov'. Alain Françon, who directed the play, succeeded in creating a simple, fast-moving production with functional sets designed by Yannis Kokkos. Françon, who founded the Théâtre Eclaté at Annecy in 1972, has a long-standing friendship with Vinaver and produced two earlier plays of his: *Les Travaux et les jours* (Annecy, 1980) and *L'Ordinaire* (Théâtre National de Chaillot, 1983). He is currently working on the première of *Portrait d'une femme*, for the 1988-9 season.

KOLTÈS

The plays of Bernard-Marie Koltès (born 1945) do not, like those of Vinaver, accept the discipline of everyday speech. They are written in highly-charged language, spinning webs of complex dramatic metaphor. These plays exhibit some of the same preoccupations as the *théâtre du quotidien:* its interest in language and in the ideological structures governing everyday speech. Yet Koltès's characters are not the halting, inarticulate creatures of many *quotidien* plays: they express themselves in fluent tirades, filled to bursting with the myths that haunt the imagination of late twentieth century western man. *Struggle of the Dogs and the Black (Combat de nègre et de chiens)* presents a kaleidoscope of myths within myths. The setting is West Africa – dark, stifling, threatening, drawing on European mythologies of fear, guilt and misunderstanding from Conrad onwards. In this setting a classic struggle is played out between 'good white' and 'bad white', the first responsible but paternalist, the second a violent drunkard, alternating between murderous aggression and childish collapse. The more they talk, the more their confrontation is revealed as a struggle of European ideologies, heightened by the African setting. Horn, the boss, is an idealist and an organisation man; he is a 'déclassé', though of working-class origins, and the only thing that can really impress him is the company he works for, with its tentacular, world-wide structure and its ability to function above the constraints of governments, politics, law and morality. He sees himself as a loyal member and servant of this 'extended family'. With this attitude goes a paternalist belief in 'co-operation', i.e., the masterminding by westerners of large engineering schemes for the good of the Third World. Cal, the engineer, is a loner: he owes allegiance to nothing. His reason for accepting foreign postings is both cynical and egotistical: they pay good money and enable him to parade his prejudices against 'inferior races'. Although the reality of West Africa gives particular shape to their conflict, this could equally well be taking place at almost any point on the globe where a Third World country is the recipient of a project funded by the World Bank. Each of these two characters employs his own rhetoric of domination; Cal's is cruder and more personal than Horn's, but both are in contradiction with the situation in which they find themselves. This situation is one of complete impotence, faced with the patient strength of Alboury the African. In the course of the action, each is obliged to recognize his impotence. The false rhetoric of the French (and European) civilizing colonial mission is gradually revealed for what it really is: a desire for power, control, ownership.

The play observes the classical unities of time, place and plot, and is unusual amongst recent French work because of its highly dramatic situation. It takes place on a construction site somewhere in West Africa and lasts through a single night from dusk until dawn. The site is dominated by the half-finished skeleton of a huge concrete road bridge; money for the project has run out and so it will never be completed. The play opens with Alboury coming in search of the body of his brother, a worker who has been killed on the site during the previous day. Cal, who it seems is responsible for his death, spends the night alternately worrying about his dog who has mysteriously disappeared, and trying in vain to recover the body of the dead African from the drain in which he has dumped it. Horn tries to placate Alboury, to calm and control Cal, and to entertain Léone, the Parisian girl whom he has persuaded to join him with a view to marriage. She becomes mesmerized by Alboury and drifts beyond the control of either Horn or Cal. In the end, Cal is shot, Léone leaves for Paris again, and Horn is left alone with nothing but the bodies of Cal and Cal's dog.

Koltès began writing plays in the 1970s, working with theatre students at Strasbourg under Jean-Pierre Vincent. He had written more than ten plays before the first two that he published. These were *Struggle of the Dogs and the Black* and *Night just before the Forest*, published together by Stock in the Théâtre Ouvert series in 1980 (and first published in translation by the Ubu Repertory Theatre of New York in 1982). *Night just before the Forest* is a long piece of dramatic monologue, first presented at the Avignon festival in 1977; *Struggle* was first produced by Patrice Chéreau at the Théâtre des Amandiers in 1984. Since then Koltès has published two more plays: *Quai*

Ouest (*Western Docks*) and *Dans la solitude des champs de coton* (*In the loneliness of the cotton fields*). Both have been produced by Chéreau at the Amandiers and both are published by Editions de Minuit. They share a setting whose context is modern America, an environment that clearly fascinates Koltès: even in *Struggle* the characters often seem to behave and speak like characters from an American film of the 1950s. For this reason, Matthew Ward's translation of the play, with its deliberate Americanisms, fits well with the tone of the original. During the 1987/8 season, Chéreau's theatre also produced Koltès's translation of *A Winter's Tale*, directed by Luc Bondy.

Chéreau's chosen style of production for Koltès's plays has often seemed to have more in common with films than theatre practice. Richard Peduzzi's design for *Struggle* faithfully reproduced an enormous concrete bridge running across the stage and all the action took place in a dusty no man's land beneath the giant legs of this fly-over. For his cast, Chéreau chose actors noted for their work in cinema as much as in theatre: Michel Piccoli played Horn, Philippe Léotard was Cal; Myriam Boyer was Léone and Sidiki Bakaba was Alboury. Where the text mentions a truck, a real vehicle was driven onto the stage and the whole production style emphasized hard realities, more reminiscent of a film set than a theatre décor. Chéreau adopted similar tactics for Koltès's second play, *Quai Ouest* (1986) set in an anonymous American dockland hangar. The same design and production team filled the stage with sections of freight containers and massive stretches of warehouse wall which moved as if possessed of a life of their own, shifting to and fro behind the actors. It is doubtful if these massive settings provided the best context for Koltès's plays. Only with his most recent production, *Dans la solitude des champs de coton* (1987) does Chéreau seem to have achieved a more appropriate, simpler style, For Koltès's work is filled with such intense and complex patterns of dramatic tension, that it is perhaps better served by productions that distract as little as possible from the relationships between the actors. Its power lies in the multiple levels of meaning at work in the dialogue, dialogue that convinces us of the particular reality of the characters, but in which we also detect the echoes of larger ideological conflicts. Through these larger conflicts, Koltès presents us with a reflection on our global village, with its struggles pitting black against white, poor against rich, the collective against the individual, the values of community against those of trade and investment. This reflection begins with something small, intensely real (the starting-point for *Struggle* was the cries of the nightwatchmen heard on a building site he visited in West Africa) and develops through central relationships of a very particular nature which nevertheless succeed in laying bare the fundamental structures of the late twentieth-century world.

COUSSE

The latest publication by Raymond Cousse (born 1942) is a slim volume written on his return from Australia in 1984. He had been invited there to perform his own version of *Stratégie pour deux jambons* (*Strategy for Two Hams*) on the occasion of the English language première of *Enfantillages*, (*These Childish Things* which, in Australia, was given the title *Kid's Stuff*). *L'Envers et l'endroit* is the diary of a humorist, a misanthropist and a self-proclaimed dilettante in the special sense of one who works only for his own enjoyment, allowing himself to be guided exclusively by his personal inclinations. Cousse is also a perfectionist, never satisfied with his own acting: he rehearses both *before* and *after* each of his performances, and these are shaped by his instincts and impulses, regardless of notions of good taste or propriety. 'For me, writing or acting are not vocations. They are what I do because I cannot conceive of any other activities.' A friend and an admirer of Beckett, who acknowledged the Frenchman's talent by publicly stating that he was 'an author with a very personal and unquestionable talent', Cousse the man is a pessimist full of despair, an anarchist without illusions who fills the void with unbounded energy, with his biting humour and, though he will not like it said, with limitless generosity. Back from Australia, disappointed by his experience, he walks the pavements of Paris and reflects in despair: 'To me my life appears like an obscenity and my vain attempts at survival like therapeutic stubbornness with myself . . . The evidence of the apocalypse was so obvious that it seemed already a thing of the past.' As for the Australians themselves, they inspired in him even darker thoughts for the whole of humanity: 'Humanity is everywhere out of place, except where crime is committed. The canker, the pox of the world.'

Before turning to the theatre, Cousse wrote novels: *Stratégie pour deux jambons* (1969–76, published 1978); *Enfantillages* (1967–72, published 1979); *Le Bâton de la Maréchale* (1978, published 1982). At the time when he began to write, he was interested in the *nouveau roman*, the theatre of the absurd and, most significantly, in Beckett, whom he met in 1968 and with whom he has corresponded ever since. His first theatrical texts were two plays for children: *La Terrine du chef* (*The Chef's Special Pâté*) and *Refus d'obtempérer* (*Refusal to obey*) and a mime play *Peripéties* (*Peripeteia*) dedicated to Beckett; all date from 1969. Two further 'acts without words' *Rencontres* (*Encounters*) and *Lever de rideau* (*Curtain raiser*) followed in 1970.

Cousse's first direct involvement with live theatre occurred in 1971, when he had to step in for an injured actor on the occasion of the première of *Peripéties*. Then, in 1979, *Stratégie pour deux jambons* was adapted for the stage at the suggestion of Christian Le Guillochet, director of the lively and adventurous Parisian centre for contemporary theatre known as Le Lucernaire. Le Guillochet persuaded Cousse to play the solo part and directed the play himself. This monologue for a pig awaiting his imminent slaughter and philosophizing about the comparative behaviour of civilized men and dirty swine had an initial run of 130 performances at the Lucernaire, where Cousse continues to revive it from time to time, and it has toured all over the world. *Stratégie* has also been translated into twenty languages, and has had over fifty different productions, making it one of the most frequently performed French plays abroad. In 1981 it played to full houses at the Avignon theatre festival, where *These Childish Things* was premièred in 1984. Cousse has now completed the stage adaptation of *Le Bâton de la Maréchale*, which he is currently rehearsing for the 1988-9 season.

These three texts, the most important that Cousse has written so far, are all monologues or, more precisely, shows for solo performers. Solo performances represent a powerful and popular trend in contemporary French theatre. At any given time, at the height of the winter season or during the lean summer months, there are several one-man or one-woman shows to be seen in Paris. The economic factor plays an important role in this trend, and the solo performance also offers well-known performers a chance to display virtuoso talents and to cash in on their fame. But neither is sufficient to explain the recent success of non-dramatic texts when transferred to the stage. In 1988, for example, two highlights of the season were solo performances of Simone de Beauvoir's *La Femme rompue* (*The Broken Woman*) at the Théâtre du Tourtour and *Le Journal d'un curé de campagne* (*Diary of a Country Priest*) by Georges Bernanos, which had a wide popular success, winning the prestigious Molière prize for 1988. It also confirmed the reputation of a great actor – Thierry Fortineau.

Cousse has commented that 'some styles of writing have a spontaneous theatrical quality; mine are of this kind. Besides I cannot conceive writing as anything other than giving three-dimensional life to language.' The act of creating language in action, either at his desk day by day, or on the stage with his body night after night, is what spurs him on. *These Childish Things*, despite its seemingly autobiographical form, does not tell a story in a realistic mode but attempts, scene by scene to get closer to the mysterious reality of childhood:

> I do not presume to recount my childhood; at most I recall the raw feelings of my first years. It is, above all, a method of composition. Allowing a child to speak – or a pig in *Stratégie* – is a way of keeping the subject in perspective. For me the written word is like music and I am only interested in the anecdote when it can be useful.

When the play was shown (in its Australian version) at the Donmar Warehouse in London (January 1988), the critics *en bloc* failed to see anything more in it than a self-indulgent exhibition devised by a 'saucy' Frenchman, although Julie Forsyth's performance was generally praised. In contrast, and despite Cousse's misgivings about Australia, the Australian theatre public and their critics were more appreciative and perceptive. Antoni Jach, for example, wrote in *The National Times* (Melbourne, 30 Nov. – 6 Dec., 1984):

> Life is seen through a keyhole; adults are ferocious – and they say things they do not mean. 'Those are only words', says the young boy imitating the priest – which leaves the boy unable to trust anything that is said in a threatening world.

DEMARCY

The work of Cousse and Richard Demarcy (also born in 1942) affords some interesting parallels and contrasts. Both work in non-mainstream theatres, Demarcy having close links with the Cartoucherie de Vincennes on the Eastern outskirts of Paris, a place which has, over the past twenty years, become the home of some of the most innovative theatre companies in France. The Théâtre du Soleil has achieved international fame, but there are also three other theatre companies working there permanently: le Théâtre de l'Epée de Bois, le Théâtre de l'Aquarium and le Théâtre de la Tempête; Demarcy collaborates with the last of these. If Cousse has an ascetic approach to theatre production and distrusts the intrusion of the spectacular, dismissing it as properly belonging to 'cinematic sub-culture', Demarcy welcomes the theatrical exploitation of the marvellous: 'Behind the theatre, either hidden or in full view, there are always the gods of the mask, i.e. the gods of Transformation and of Metamorphosis.' Both writers share a profound dissatisfaction with the world as it is; but Cousse's despair is metaphysical and accepts no palliative, whereas Demarcy, with sober optimism and theatrical playfulness, is ready to give the future a chance.

L'Étranger dans la maison (*Stranger in the House*), first performed by the Théâtre de la Tempête in 1982 in Demarcy's own production, was his eighth play and as many again have been written and performed since. His most recent works are *Voyages d'hiver* (*Winter Trips*, Théâtre de l'Athénée, Paris, 1986), *La Grotte d'Ali* (*Ali's Cave*, Opéra de Lyon, 1986), *Les Rêves de Lolita et Laverdure* (*Lolita's Dreams and Laverdure*, Théâtre 14–J. Marie-Serreau, Paris, 1987), *Les deux bossus* (*The Two Hunchbacks*, Lyon, 1987). With the collaboration of his wife, Teresa Motta, he also writes in Portuguese and directs in Portugal (in 1975-6, they wrote and performed *Fables théâtrales sur la révolution portugaise* [*Theatre Tales on the Portuguese Revolution*] in Paris and Lisbon). In both countries Teresa Motta works closely with Demarcy and she performs in both languages. Richard Demarcy is also a distinguished academic. He teaches in the Department of Theatre Studies (Institut de Recherches Théâtrales) at the University of Paris III (Censier-Sorbonne nouvelle). In 1973 he published an important study on the role of live entertainment in contemporary western society, *Éléments d'une sociologie du spectacle* (Éditions 10/18).

Demarcy finds his inspiration in everyday life. He is constantly aware of the realities of the economic, political and social situation surrounding him and his aim is to bear witness to the injustices and iniquities in the world. But he pursues his aim as a magician of the theatre and finds his inspiration in the huge patrimony of popular nursery rhymes, laments, soldier songs, old-wives tales, saws, and so on – sources of inspiration which are the common stock of writers all over the world. As it happens, *Stranger in the House* uses at the centre of its fable some folklore elements which Peter Weiss also employed in a short play *Nacht mit Gästen* (*Guests in the Night*) written in 1963. A comparison between the two plays highlights the different usage of similar elements and helps to stress Demarcy's optimistic outlook as opposed to Weiss's (and Cousse's) despairing view of mankind. The starting point is the same in both plays: an 'ordinary' family is getting ready for bed when an 'uninvited guest' forces his way in and thus unleashes a chain of extraordinary events. The German play is uncompromisingly bleak and humourless, set as it is in some existential limbo. It is, in short, a product of the 'theatre of the absurd': the 'guest' comes over as a kind of disembodied Macheath, or death figure, whose sole purpose is to sow murder and destruction. The author clearly states that in production one must 'stress the evil, malevolent, anguished, devilish aspects' of the character. Weiss's stranger falls on the family like an exterminating scourge, without rhyme or reason, but simply because in Weiss's philosophy such a relationship between a cruel and senseless tormentor and his victims is paradigmatic of all human relationships, now and forever.

In contrast, Demarcy's comedy is firmly rooted in the rich soil of contemporary French society, with all its strengths and failings. Long before the 1988 presidential elections, which gave the fascists of Le Pen a staggering 16% of votes, racialism and anti-semitism were perceived as two real dangers to the civic health of French society.

Even when treated as light-heartedly as in *L'Étranger dans la maison* the subject of
racism stirs up antagonisms and many theatres refused Demarcy access to their stage.
In Demarcy's play the stranger is not a mythical being, but a real individual, although
a figment of the imagination of the other characters, since the whole action, until the
last scene, is an extended dream sequence. The stranger, then, is one of those many
coloured immigrants (from Algeria, Morocco, Tunisia . . . , from other former French
colonies) who fulfil the thankless and indispensable jobs which French men and
women refuse to consider. These 'immigrants', the vast majority of whom were born
in France and are French citizens, are commonly referred to as 'les étrangers' ('the
foreigners') and kept at arm's length. Of course France is not South Africa, but it is
not only the members of the National Front who feel a visceral hatred towards the
children of the former colonized peoples. The family whose nightmare the stranger
inhabits pretends to normality, although they happily bump one another off, for no
good reason. Murder here is as joyful, and as chilling, as in Georges Michel's *La
Promenade du dimanche (The Sunday Walk)*. At the opening of the play, the parents
are lumbered with the corpse of one of their children, whereas the surviving brats
have despatched grandad who stiffens in the cupboard. Two cumbersome parcels, but
they will come in handy at a later stage. When the stranger bursts into this unlikely
scene, he turns out to be quite different from the murderous 'sex-maniac wog' of the
father's imagination, just as, in the face of adversity, the father fails to display the
virtues which he himself would expect from an 'upright citizen'. It is their mother –
who has an untold number of children – who seduces the 'blackamoor' herself and
thereby finds love and sexual fulfilment for the first time in her life. Or she would,
were the King of France, strangely reminiscent of Mitterrand's predecessor, Giscard
d'Estaing, not to come in uninvited to share a sumptuous dinner with an 'ordinary
family'. Although Giscard d'Estaing had suffered electoral defeat by the time the play
was performed, the scene has lost none of its satirical strength and would work equally
well in another political context.

The device of setting the play within the context of a dream, like Howard Brenton's
Thirteenth Night, does not weaken the impact of the fable. Quite the contrary, since
Demarcy seems to signal that the portrayal of a 'stranger' as a positive hero still
remains in the realm of utopia. One will have to wait for the children to grow up and
for the beneficial effects of the dream to operate, before a fundamental change of
mentality can be expected and for segregation to become a thing of the past.

David Bradby
Claude Schumacher

REFERENCE
1. *Le Compte Rendu d'Avignon: Des mille maux dont souffre l'édition théâtrale et des
trente-sept remèdes pour l'en soulager* by Michel Vinaver, Actes Sud with the *Centre
National des Lettres*, 1987.

NOTE
This is the first collection of new French plays to be published in Britain for many
years; it has been made possible by a grant from the French Embassy Cultural
Services in London. It follows a successful set of readings arranged under the auspices
of M. Michel Monory, director of the French Institute in London, and held at the
Riverside Studios, Hammersmith, in 1986. We are indebted to the Ubu Repertory
Theatre of New York for making the translations of *Struggle of the Dogs and the
Black* and *Stranger in the House* available to us.

PORTRAIT OF A WOMAN

Translated by Donald Watson

MICHEL VINAVER has written over a dozen plays and is widely recognized as France's foremost playwright. His work has been directed by, among others, Roger Planchon (*Les Coréens*, 1956, and *Par-dessus bord*, 1973), Antoine Vitez (*Iphigénie Hotel*, 1977) and Jacques Lassalle (*Dissident* and *Nina*, 1976, and *A la renverse*, 1979). His most recent work has been directed partly by himself and partly by Alain Françon (*L'Ordinaire*, 1981; *Les Voisins*, 1986). In 1987 Sam Walters directed *A Smile at the End of the Line*, translated from *Les Travaux et les jours* by Peter Meyer. Vinaver has written adaptations of *The Shoemakers Holiday* by Dekker, *The Suicide* by Erdmann, and *Summerfolk* by Gorki. *Portrait of a Woman* published here in a translation by Donald Watson, is Vinaver's most recent play. It has seventeen characters but is written to be performed by eleven actors. It is due to be premièred in France in 1988/9, directed by Alain Françon.

Characters

SOPHIE AUZANNEAU ⎫
XAVIER BERGERET ⎪
CORNAILLE   ⎬ *medical students*
LACHAUD   ⎪
CLAUDETTE   ⎭
COLONNA, *on the teaching staff of the Faculty of Medicine*
Monsieur AUZANNEAU
Madame AUZANNEAU
Madame GUIBOT, *Sophie Auzanneau's landlady*
DR BERND SCHLESSINGER, *surgeon*
GERBIER, *gunsmith*
FRANCINE, *Xavier Bergeret's fiancée*
The PRESIDENT *of the Court of Assizes in Paris*
The PUBLIC PROSECUTOR
Maître LUBET, *Counsel for the Plaintiff*
Maître CANCÉ, *Counsel for the Defence*
Dr HAUDEBOURG, *expert*

The following parts are played by one performer:
– M. AUZANNEAU, THE GUNSMITH, DR SCHLESSINGER
– Mme AUZANNEAU, Mme GUIBOT
– LACHAUD, DR HAUDEBOURG
– CORNAILLE, COLONNA
– FRANCINE, CLAUDETTE

A circular or oval stage with no fixed décor. A stagehand, in constant attendance, is ready as the action unfolds to introduce, remove or change round the portable items of the setting. These are of two strongly contrasted types. On the one hand the chairs, tables, beds, doors etc. belonging to the outside world . . . monochrome, undifferentiated, inexpressive and interchangeable, blending together to serve various functions, brought on or taken off only as the need arises. On the other hand the ultra-realistic representation of the Court of Assizes in Paris in 1953; or rather a fragmentary suggestion of it, isolated pieces of an unfinished jigsaw puzzle, each one executed in trompe-l'œil. *Human figures can be represented in these items (assessors, clerk of the court, guards, jurymen, photographers, journalists, the general public), which never leave the stage though they are subject to continual rearrangement, by sudden changes or by smooth transition, to create an impression of constant movement.*

A soundtrack intermittently reproduces the mutterings, laughter, exclamations and disruptions from the public.

Eleven actors take seventeen parts. The changes of appearance (costume, hairpieces etc.) needed for the five actors playing more than one role are made swiftly and perfunctorily in full view of the audience.

The play is continuous and is performed without an interval.

It opens with the appearance of the stagehand, who brings on a landing door and installs it in the centre of the stage. On one side of the door is the staircase of an apartment block; on the other, where the stagehand places a chair and an armchair on either side of a table, is Xavier's bedsitter, 25 rue de l'Abbé Groult, Paris XVe, on the seventh floor. Xavier comes and sits in the armchair. Pause.
SOPHIE *appears on the landing.*

PRESIDENT. She walked up to the seventh floor
Why didn't you use the lift?

Mme GUIBOT. Forewarned is forearmed
What's more the boy was warned twice two telegrams the same day one from me and one from his dad

PRESIDENT. Your telegram despatched from Lille on the 15th of March was couched in the following terms 'Sophie gone to Paris stop avoid meeting urgent'

Mme GUIBOT. Better safe than sorry Mr President so I warned his dad as well

PRESIDENT. And the same day the father sent the following telegram to his son 'return immediately Saint-Omer'

SOPHIE *rings at the door.* XAVIER *waits for a time, stands up, moves to the door, hesitates, then opens it.* SOPHIE *enters the room.*

XAVIER. What are you doing here?

SOPHIE. I had to see you

SOPHIE *moves quickly forward and sits on the chair.* XAVIER *returns to his armchair.*

XAVIER. I told you we shouldn't see each other any more

PRESIDENT. Several remarks were exchanged more or less in the same vein

SOPHIE. I couldn't not see you again things I've got to explain

XAVIER. There's nothing left for us to say you know

SOPHIE. I can't help it you've got to hear me out
Listen

XAVIER. What difference will it make?

SOPHIE. I can't

XAVIER. Listen Sophie that's the way it is

SOPHIE. What way?

XAVIER. It's all over

SOPHIE *takes a revolver from her raincoat pocket and fires to hit him in the forehead.* XAVIER *collapses over the table. She stands up and shoots him in the back. Then she fires a third time, into his ear.*

SOPHIE. I walked up to the seventh floor because I needed time to think out what I had to tell him find the right words to use I hoped if I knew how to talk to him I could make him feel sorry and win him over

PRESIDENT. And failing that put an end to him and then commit suicide?

She nods her head slowly in confirmation.

Only you forgot
In your disturbed state
To turn the weapon on yourself

MAÎTRE LUBET. Understandably Monsieur le Président what else can one expect? In the heat of the moment one can't think of everything

SOPHIE. Face to face I couldn't say any of the things I wanted to
He seemed so distant
Almost a stranger

LUBET. So you might as well have taken the lift

SOPHIE. It happened so quickly
It was over before I realized
I was so worked up

PRESIDENT. You know how to fire a gun
One bullet at zero range the other two point-blank

PUBLIC PROSECUTOR. Yes he collapses the first time you fire but do you then put your arm around him and cry 'Xavier speak to me what have I done?'
No you aim a second shot into his back do your nerves get the better of you?
No you fire a final bullet at zero range into his ear
And this Sophie Auzanneau and I'm appalled to have to say it to a young girl like you
This is what you did and didn't do

LUBET. How did you deliver the fatal shot? What position was he in? Head slumped over like this? Or like this?

SOPHIE. I can't give you the details sir if I could remember I'd tell you

LUBET. Hm and after that?
You were found on the kitchen floor with the gas turned on
Oh yes a revolver's too brutal you prefer gas you know all about that from your medical studies that there's not so much risk lying flat on the floor and you hadn't forgotten

MAÎTRE CANCÉ. I deny the implication that between the three

shots there was breathing space to think
That was a mean suggestion
Cheap and cruel
It was murder that's true she meant to kill and she did isn't that enough for you?
No you have to turn it into a novelette distort the facts and serve them up like a fisherman's yarn

Mme GUIBOT. Still he had been warned

PRESIDENT. Forewarned as he was how do you explain that he opened the door?

Mme GUIBOT. He was a young gentleman none better nice as they come
Well brought up good manners

PRESIDENT. He knew he was at risk

LACHAUD. He was on his guard but perhaps deep down he wasn't
He passed the telegram on to me and said 'here take it if anything happens to me you can prove there was malice aforethought' but whether he believed it or not

PRESIDENT. He didn't follow his father's advice which reads more like an order 'return immediately Saint-Omer'

LACHAUD. Xavier was anything but chicken

CORNAILLE. But those telegrams were on his mind he spent the last two days of his life rather like someone on the run

LACHAUD. He stuck close to his friends either sleeping at their place or persuading them to come to his

CORNAILLE. She managed to catch up with him she wanted to see him tête-à-tête he put the meeting off made a date in the Place de l'Odéon for the 17th at 9.45

PRESIDENT. But persistent as she was she posted herself the previous evening in a café opposite No. 25 rue de l'Abbé Groult

PUBLIC PROSECUTOR Sees him come home walks up to his apartment with the revolver in her coat pocket

PRESIDENT. Sophie Auzanneau after

you recovered consciousness when the police questioned you you declared 'all I know is I took my revolver out to kill myself in front of Xavier but I can't remember anything that happened from the moment the first shot went off'
Do you still stick to this version of the facts?

SOPHIE. No

PRESIDENT. And what is today's version?

SOPHIE. It's not a version, sir
I wanted to kill us both yes at the time I mean to bring him down with me both of us together

LUBET. You no longer maintain you killed Bergeret by accident?

SOPHIE. No

LUBET. So you lied to the police?

SOPHIE. Yes

LUBET. Yet today you're indignant if we cast doubt on a single word you say on this matter Sir I have nothing more to add
Except that in your shoes Sophie Auzanneau I'd show a little less indignation and a great deal more remorse

SOPHIE. You're not in my shoes

LUBET. For you will have noticed Ladies and Gentlemen of the Jury that nothing the defendant has said so far

CANCÉ. I protest Monsieur le Président

LUBET. Betrays the slightest trace of remorse

PRESIDENT. I must have order in the Court
I will not hesitate if the need arises to suspend this hearing
I will ensure come what may that these proceedings be conducted in an orderly manner
I ask the defendant

The terrace of a café in Lille.

SOPHIE. Me? What do I like?
To be always changing new situations like a boy following you when a lecture's over

XAVIER. That's not very new
There aren't hundreds of new situations
You can count them on the fingers of one hand three or four at the most
Each with a number of variations

SOPHIE. The number of situations is infinite
And each time the world begins again

XAVIER. A world like that would be unthinkable

SOPHIE. What good does thinking do?

XAVIER. To grasp things

SOPHIE. To let them grasp you

XAVIER. To be passive?

SOPHIE. To drift

XAVIER. Anywhere?

SOPHIE. Wherever

XAVIER. That's what you believe?

SOPHIE. Chance and fate are two sides of the same coin

XAVIER. I believe one can and should take control of one's life

SOPHIE. What for?

XAVIER. To get somewhere

SOPHIE. Are you serious?

XAVIER. I don't mean a career or happiness maybe what I mean is the image you have of yourself

SOPHIE. My elder brother was drowned in his submarine
The younger one died in his fighter plane a few months later on an exercise it crashed

XAVIER. What's that got to do with it?

SOPHIE. There's such a gap between us

XAVIER. Perhaps that's why I wanted to follow you

SOPHIE. What about cats? Do you like black cats? A black cat stalking through the long grass?

XAVIER. Where are you from? If you don't mind my asking?

SOPHIE. My family live in the suburbs of Dunkirk I was born in Dunkirk a town that was a fort
Inert they talk about the force of inertia don't they? You're very polite

Do you like long beaches?
I love pebbles all kinds of stones
I pick them up fill my pockets with them
I'd like to break them open to see what's inside

XAVIER. Shall we have supper together this evening?

SOPHIE. Do I interest you? I must find out about you what you like. I bet you love kicking a ball about you look like a striker you do play football? Where's your family from?

XAVIER. My father's a vet at Arras
I'm not a bad cook you can come to my place

SOPHIE. All the boys I meet want to cook for me
It's a stroke of luck because I
But I've got some revision to do

XAVIER. We'll revise together

SOPHIE. Will you ask me some stinkers about the cervical vertebrae?

XAVIER. Or the iliac bone

SOPHIE. It's such a huge subject

XAVIER. Colonna does his best to make a shambles of it

SOPHIE. Oh him and his urinary tract he's fanatical about it
The urethra I ask you and the bladder what a bore I easily get swamped

XAVIER. All depends on the prof
Colonna's hard to follow
I'll grill you some sardines

SOPHIE. I hate sardines
Specially oven-grilled with mustard my mother's favourite dish the smell lingers in the house all year round

At the Auzanneaus' house in the suburbs of Dunkirk.

Mme AUZANNEAU. That storm's played havoc with the garden

SOPHIE. It doesn't really matter you know

Mme AUZANNEAU. Reminds me of the storm we had when our little girl left home and we only found out later she'd gone to the hospital to become a nurse

XAVIER. You're on bad terms with her?

SOPHIE. This all sounds like the start of a novel

M. AUZANNEAU. And a tart

Mme AUZANNEAU. How do we know what went on? She wasn't even seventeen and he was at least fifty-five

M. AUZANNEAU. What are we eating?

Mme AUZANNEAU. A nice tail-end of cod
Fresh from market this morning
At least that Schlessinger was a decent sort of chap who made sure she had proper meals

In a bar in Paris.

FRANCINE. I've been so scared

Mme AUZANNEAU. She hadn't even stopped growing

M. AUZANNEAU. A disaster for the beans

Mme AUZANNEAU. And those hailstones
The tomatoes all peppered with them

FRANCINE. You you're always so punctual
Oh Xavier I imagined all sorts of things
I thought she must have tracked you down

M. AUZANNEAU. She was sixteen when she took off and that was the start because you put up with all her shenanigans
I must go and prop up that pear tree

At the gunsmith's in Lille.

SOPHIE. How much is that one?

Mme AUZANNEAU. It would be the one with the best pears
But she'll settle down again
It's the times we live in
The war

SOPHIE. And that one?
I know nothing about them you know
To fire it

GUNSMITH. First you load it

SOPHIE. Yes of course you load it

XAVIER. Poor darling
But I don't want to keep you in the
dark
She found me and I'm sure it wasn't by
accident she knew my movements
It's hopeless you get the feeling you
can't get through to her with words

FRANCINE. And then?
After that?

XAVIER. I told her about you and me

GUNSMITH. Take a good look

FRANCINE. When you're jealous you
don't listen

XAVIER. To be jealous you have to be
in love she doesn't love me

FRANCINE. I'm not so sure all I know
is that you don't love her because you
love me
You do love me?

XAVIER. Sure as this table's a table

FRANCINE. Fancy comparing

XAVIER. I'm not comparing you to the
table

FRANCINE. You're comparing our love
to a table

SOPHIE. And what does one do next?

XAVIER. All I mean is our love is as
real as this table
My love

FRANCINE. I thought it was stronger
than that
Never mind what did she want?

GUNSMITH. That's it then you take aim

SOPHIE. Nothing too complicated

GUNSMITH. What matters is how you
look after it
If you want it to give you good service
You make a weapon last by taking
good care of it
This pistol here see made in 1780 it's
always been in the Bonachon family
we've been gunsmiths since 1720.

SOPHIE. Are you a Bonachon?

GUNSMITH. Yes and no I married a
Bonachon
My name's Gerbier but Bonachon's
still the firm's name

You've got a licence?

SOPHIE. You need a licence?

GUNSMITH. I'd advise you to choose
this one
It's easier to handle

Mme GUIBOT. She showed me her
revolver sir oh she never kept nothing
from me not a bit sly no almost the
opposite

PRESIDENT. Meaning what?

Mme GUIBOT. If she had a bee in her
bonnet she went overboard

PRESIDENT. But she didn't go over the
top for this boy

Mme GUIBOT. Not to start with

PRESIDENT. At the start it was
Bergeret who was mad about her

Mme GUIBOT. Yes

LUBET. The fact that she wasn't so keen
on Bergeret
Didn't stop her slipping between his
sheets
But she didn't mind changing her
sheets did she?
It's even said she could do without
sheets
The oilcloth on a kitchen table would
do

PRESIDENT. Order

LUBET. I have here a letter addressed
to her by one of her former lovers in
which allusion is clearly made to the
corner of a kitchen table covered with
a pink and white oilcloth.

CANCÉ. All is grist to my learned
friend's mill even if he risks
contradicting his own argument
If there had been intent wouldn't my
client have taken care before
committing the crime to destroy this
intimate correspondence the contents
of which could clearly be used against
her?
The bare facts speak for themselves but
you no you have to spice them up and
so mask their authentic flavour
Too spicy by half
It's unfair to single out one sentence
What I want you to arrive at Members
of the Jury is a total view of a complex
human being of a whole live person
who merits your understanding

however guilty she may be but you must remain cool and curb your abhorrence if you are to listen attentively to the innermost promptings of her heart
Hard as it is for you to enter this emotional arena here alone is there a chance some answer may emerge to the fearful question you have to resolve
Why did she do it?

LUBET. Self-interest as I shall demonstrate
For want of any argument he can get his teeth in my esteemed colleague is riding a fashionable hobby-horse in-depth psychology which as we know will permit him to make any claim he likes even to call a black cat white
Why do I speak of a black cat? We have evidence according to which the defendant had a passion for a black cat
No doubt her one and only genuine passion
But apart from that my learned friend we know how predisposed you are to dredge everything up from the vertiginous depths of the soul
Petty of me perhaps but I'm concerned with the facts
I stick to the facts

SOPHIE's *room in Lille.*

Mme GUIBOT. Like the butcher fr'instance he's all upset waiting for his bill to be paid
'Course *I* don't complain about you only you owe me the last two months' rent
My sunniest room I only have one per floor with two windows and you've got the top one looks over the trees
The one everyone asks for
You must say if you want to stay

XAVIER. She threatened to kill me I mean she made a scene

Mme GUIBOT. If you're staying it's all right by me

FRANCINE. Did you love her very much?

Mme GUIBOT. I've got used to you

XAVIER. For me she was a demon

Mme GUIBOT. Even if you've got lots

of things on your mind and not all of them nice ones
You mustn't forget to pay me

FRANCINE. More than me? Did you love her more than me?

Mme GUIBOT. If you're staying
You're always tearing from place to place

XAVIER. It hurts me that love can come to an end

Mme GUIBOT. No good tormenting yourself like this

FRANCINE. Hers?

XAVIER. Mine
'Cos she never loved *me*

Mme GUIBOT. You ought to empty your head of this rubbish for good an' all

XAVIER. When I broke with her she was annoyed not upset
That's what my friends told me

FRANCINE. One day you might stop loving me too?

XAVIER. With those big round glasses of yours
My sweet angel

FRANCINE. Aren't you scared?

XAVIER. You know I'm not
I ought to be
Cornaille thinks if I don't clear off abroad for six months without leaving an address

SOPHIE. No I can't marry you

XAVIER. Why?

SOPHIE. Deep down I'm sure of it you you're so positive

XAVIER. So what?

SOPHIE. So stable so clear
I'm staying Madame Guibot I'm staying

Mme GUIBOT. Just as well just as well you're in no state too much running through that head of yours and you can't go on like this on an empty stomach
Two days you've gone without food

XAVIER. I try to reason myself into being scared

Mme GUIBOT. You must eat

SOPHIE. I can't

XAVIER. But you know

Mme GUIBOT. A cup of tea and some chocolate biscuits I bought you

XAVIER. It's my weakness I believe everyone is naturally good

SOPHIE; I can't marry you

FRANCINE. Go away if you have to Don't give your address even to me not to anyone I'll wait a year for you two years

XAVIER. It was Lachaud slipped her my address
She was waiting for me outside the Faculty she'd checked up she knew what time I came out

Mme GUIBOT. For two days now you've been shut in your room Curled up in a ball on your bed

FRANCINE. Xavier oh Xavier listen All sorts of ideas are rushing through my mind

Mme GUIBOT. Shut him out of your heart Mademoiselle Sophie once and for all if you'll take my advice

SOPHIE. I can't

Mme GUIBOT. And in three or six months you'll see you'll be a different person

SOPHIE. He's dug his claws into me

FRANCINE. When you come back we'll open your surgery can you see me in a white coat? I'll note down your appointments you'd like me to be your assistant? At the start we'll be living from hand to mouth but then

SOPHIE. I feel as if I'm sinking

FRANCINE. You'll see and even When we've had time to build up a practice

Mme GUIBOT. You like them these little biscuits? Come on it'll all work out in time

SOPHIE. I can't hang on any longer I'll end up doing something dreadful

Mme GUIBOT. That's what she said

SOPHIE. I don't care if I'm not a good loser I don't love him enough to watch him walk off with somebody else

Mme GUIBOT. And she showed me her gun she held out her arm

CANCÉ. Do you think of her as a cold-blooded criminal?

Mme GUIBOT. And she went and took it from under her pillow
And brandished it in my face and she told me
If you want my opinion she's not all there maybe she does put on an act but she gets too caught up in the part she's playing and then she overdoes it

SOPHIE. What fate decrees that must we blindly obey

At the Auzanneaus' in Dunkirk

Mme AUZANNEAU. It's no use
Your answer's always the same

CANCÉ. She's meant to be hard-hearted

M. AUZANNEAU. Because it's always the same old story

Mme AUZANNEAU. When we first met it wasn't like this

CANCÉ. But underneath the armour she's built up

M. AUZANNEAU. It was exactly the same

Mme AUZANNEAU. You saw me in a different light
It's no use

CANCÉ. A poor heart was desperately beating

M. AUZANNEAU. If we've got to go back that far
I saw you as the sweet little darling you were

Mme AUZANNEAU. Like the sweet little darlings you ogle today when they walk past under the window

CANCÉ. Locked away in prison

M. AUZANNEAU. Haven't you done enough nagging? What is it you want? For us to go out dancing? We'll do some jiving Ha ha ha
Tomorrow for our little girl's birthday Any of that stew left over?
You ought to give us sardines
It's a long time

Mme AUZANNEAU. Tomorrow

M. AUZANNEAU. Our little girl loves them

Mme AUZANNEAU. What about the present?

M. AUZANNEAU. How many years has she been telling us not to put ourselves out for her

Mme AUZANNEAU. It's true with her we could never get it right

M. AUZANNEAU. What we did last year three thousand francs in an envelope she never turns her nose up at that

Mme AUZANNEAU. This year Louis you could make it five thousand everything's so expensive

At the gunsmith's in Lille.

SOPHIE. How much does it cost?

Mme AUZANNEAU. It's her brothers she's missing you know

GUNSMITH. Four thousand eight hundred

SOPHIE. Oh I've not got enough

A bistro in Lille.

CORNAILLE. Cut your losses

LACHAUD. The bloody fool's blubbing.

GUNSMITH. How much have you got without indiscretion?

SOPHIE. Two thousand five hundred

GUNSMITH. If you cross the road there's a toyshop where they sell water-pistols

CORNAILLE. What good does crying do? Belt her one
Take your choice either you belt her give her a beating she won't forget or you say cheerio hello and goodbye Sophie best of luck with Colonna

LACHAUD. Give her the push

XAVIER. But I'm crazy about her

CORNAILLE. A damn good hiding then Because she's taking you for a ride

PRESIDENT. So it was then you set your cap at Xavier Bergeret
A decent young man clever and ambitious
From a close-knit family well regarded in Saint-Omer
Answer me

SOPHIE. Yes Monsieur le Président

LACHAUD. The way she flaunts herself

CORNAILLE. The three of us'll gang up and bash her about

LACHAUD. Like a tart

PRESIDENT. His father was a vet a man of means

LACHAUD. Beat her up

CORNAILLE. If you let it drag on

PRESIDENT. A good choice
A comfortable prospect for you gilt-edged no?

SOPHIE. Yes Monsieur le Président

LACHAUD. She plays the field to get up your nose

CORNAILLE. It's not Colonna she's after
What she wants is to watch you getting all screwed up while she makes a play for Colonna

PRESIDENT. In other words you had everything to make you happy

LACHAUD. For the whole world to see

SOPHIE. I don't know

PRESIDENT. Nor presumably do you know the reason why
When you had found someone to love you
You gave in to this Monsieur Colonna?

LACHAUD. That's the way she loves you

CORNAILLE. She'll be the death of you

LACHAUD. Stop being a bloody fool Xavier

XAVIER. It would be easy if she was only aiming this at me
For some reason I don't understand she's doing it
To hurt herself

SOPHIE. I don't know

CORNAILLE. A good hiding

XAVIER. I don't think

CORNAILLE. That's what she's asking for

PRESIDENT. You don't know?
Let's say it's a classic ploy for a woman
Jealousy fans the flame you can find
examples of it in all the best authors
can't you?

XAVIER. To drift

SOPHIE. I don't know

PRESIDENT. But you've told us you
devoured all kinds of novels perched
up there in your pear tree

XAVIER. The first time I met her she
told me that's what she liked to drift

LACHAUD. What she needed as a kid
was
A proper dad
I'm not sure but you can imagine
If he'd given her the odd spanking she
was after

At the Auzanneaus' in Dunkirk.

Mme AUZANNEAU. You look peaky
Sophie
You getting enough to eat?

LACHAUD. That's what she wants from
you

CORNAILLE. She's dying for it

Mme AUZANNEAU. Since last year
you've lost weight
But as we only see you on your
birthday

M. AUZANNEAU. You tell her that
every time

Mme AUZANNEAU. You don't take
enough care of yourself

M. AUZANNEAU. Off we go again

Mme AUZANNEAU. What?

M. AUZANNEAU. It's no use

SOPHIE. I've been working hard mum

Mme AUZANNEAU. If we saw a little
more of you

SOPHIE. I paid you a visit in September
did you forget?

Mme AUZANNEAU. A flying visit

XAVIER. It's not in my nature

SOPHIE. To pick up my winter things

LACHAUD. Later will be too late

CORNAILLE. It's now or never

XAVIER. The moment's neither here
nor there it's not like that with her

Mme AUZANNEAU. You don't look
well
Do you get enough sleep?
You should come and spend part of the
summer here to build yourself up again

LACHAUD. The shrew's asking to be
tamed

SOPHIE. They failed me in my exam

CORNAILLE. Tame her or chuck her
out

M. AUZANNEAU. And you say you've
been working?

SOPHIE. Looks as if you've redone the
roof

XAVIER. Sophie's beautiful inside and
out

M. AUZANNEAU. The gale blew half
of it away

XAVIER. She's fighting against God
knows what

M. AUZANNEAU. Nothing left of the
beans
The pear tree

Mme AUZANNEAU. And the tomatoes

XAVIER. Struggling against something
inside her that's breaking her up

M. AUZANNEAU. The storm split the
pear tree in two

XAVIER. It's got nothing to do with her
nature
Sophie's not a nympho she hasn't got it
in her

SOPHIE. My pear tree?

M. AUZANNEAU. To say nothing
about the others

CORNAILLE. You must snap out of
your dreamworld

Mme AUZANNEAU. And you're still
seeing that boy?

LACHAUD. She's screwing with
Colonna

SOPHIE. Xavier he got through

CORNAILLE. Colonna's a better bet than you are

SOPHIE. I'm sitting it again next session
In the spring we're getting married setting up in Paris
Doctor Xavier and Doctor Sophie Bergeret
Sound good?
I want to go and see the pear tree
You didn't cut it down?

Mme AUZANNEAU. Well say something why don't you tell her?
Dad managed to save it the trunk was split all the way down he put a clamp round it

M. AUZANNEAU. We'll have to wait till spring

Mme AUZANNEAU. Give her the envelope
Oh Louis why don't you tell her for once?
For your twenty-fourth birthday here's an envelope you really deserve it because you've worked hard

M. AUZANNEAU. So hard they failed her
Ha ha ha

Mme AUZANNEAU. Don't pay attention to your father's little jokes you know him and if you get married There'll be something else on top of it of course

PRESIDENT. At that precise moment Sophie Auzanneau did you love him?

SOPHIE. I don't know

PRESIDENT. I doubt it will do you any good to retreat into silence

SOPHIE. I say what I know

PRESIDENT. The Court is trying to understand

Mme AUZANNEAU. That way when we're old *you* won't forget *us* in our old age

PRESIDENT. You're anxious for us to believe you
So give us an exact account of how your relationship with Xavier Bergeret began

SOPHIE. He followed me
He suggested we went for a drink
He invited me back to his place to

have some fresh grilled sardines
I told him I wasn't too keen on his sardines

PRESIDENT. At your very first meeting a certain pattern was established in the contact between you
You switch him on then you switch him off in a game of cat and mouse

SOPHIE. I was talking about sardines
He was quite put out he didn't know what to do with his hands so I pressed them over my breasts and then we went to his place to go to bed

PRESIDENT. Was it he who proposed this?

SOPHIE. I don't remember

PRESIDENT. Whichever way it was you weren't embarrassed? Spending the night with a young man you'd never seen before that day?

SOPHIE. It was pleasure

PRESIDENT. Pleasure comes easily to you
I insist on order in this Court
You take your pleasure with Bergeret pleasure with Colonna then with Legouit and I pass over the others
I suppose when you were sixteen Colonel Schlessinger the Doctor in the German army gave you pleasure just as easily

Mme AUZANNEAU. Your Papa has sacrificed a lot for you and you've never given him a single word of thanks
He doesn't ask for much
When he patched that pear tree together who do you think he did it for?
Who does the work that pays for your room in Lille your registration fees your dissecting instruments and all those books and dictionaries?
When we sent your elder brother to university he wrote us this letter I've always kept and I must have read it to you a hundred times

The bed in XAVIER's *room in Lille.*

SOPHIE. It was the tree I used to climb

when I was small I'd stay there for
hours curled up in the fork where the
three big branches met
My cat used to come too when she felt
like it and snuggle down in my lap I'd
tickle her behind the ears and when *I*
felt like it I'd pick a pear that still
wasn't ripe and dig my teeth in
There in my nest I was invincible

XAVIER. Invisible you mean

SOPHIE. Invincible because I was out of
sight

XAVIER. You've always like to remain
unseen
Yet you'll get up to anything to draw
attention to yourself?

SOPHIE. It's bliss
To hide myself away
No Xavier
I don't love you as much as you love
me

PRESIDENT. He insisted you should
marry him

XAVIER. You play hide and seek with
yourself
You hide from your own feelings
I can see what you refuse to see

SOPHIE. What do you see?

XAVIER. That you love me
I'll make you see it
We'll get married and you'll see

SOPHIE. I don't know

XAVIER. The ice will melt

SOPHIE. You'll be my tree

XAVIER. Will you then?

SOPHIE. And the storm will come

XAVIER. You're devastating

DR HAUDEBOURG. She betrays a
particular form of instability which is
the signal characteristic of an
unbalanced mind she's impulsive
irascible and if you add to that strong
signs of degeneration on the maternal
side of her family

SOPHIE. I don't want to make you
unhappy

DR HAUDEBOURG. The
concomitance of these two observations
has led us to the conclusion that this is
a case of diminished responsibility

XAVIER. I want to make you happy

PUBLIC PROSECUTOR. She has told
us Doctor that she fired in cold blood
you speak of her 'irascibility' how did
you get that idea?

DR HAUDEBOURG. Let's call it 'an
irascible state of mind' it makes no
difference she is irascible by nature but
may still maintain a certain coolness in
any given act
Psychiatry anyway is not a
mathematical science

SOPHIE. You're so terribly tender and
gentle with me

XAVIER. And you don't like it?

SOPHIE. I'm not used to it
Are you taking me to a film
I want to smooch at the flicks

XAVIER. You're still not giving me an
answer

SOPHIE. Afterwards we'll see

LUBET. So we can see Members of the
Jury that even before the fatal act of
physical liquidation
There was a deliberate attempt at
psychological degradation the breaking
down of a human being whose one
weakness was an attachment to certain
values
A precious metal that will be attacked
insidiously by an acid which will prove
fatal to it

Mme GUIBOT. She was a chilly mortal
too
Not a mollycoddle I mean there's a
difference she used to roll herself up
without a stitch on in three thick
blankets even in the summer
Her cat in bed with her
And giggle

COLONNA's *bedroom in Lille.*

XAVIER. I'm intruding on your privacy
Monsieur Colonna

COLONNA. What can I do for you
Bergeret?
At this hour I must say

Mme GUIBOT. Sometimes there were
two or three people in her room peals
of laughter and hers was the loudest

XAVIER. Is Sophie here?

COLONNA. I'm sorry Sophie who?

XAVIER. Sophie Auzanneau

COLONNA. Auzanneau? What an idea

XAVIER. It's about her I've come to see
you
She's been seen with you quite a lot
she doesn't hide it
I'm interested in her it's not a secret
we've been together for over a year I
want to know what's going on
I have a right to know

COLONNA. Ask her

XAVIER. She says she's a free agent

COLONNA. If that's what she thinks

XAVIER. But you see it's not what she
thinks she tells me

COLONNA. What can I do about it?

XAVIER. You can tell me if you love
her if you're thinking of marriage

COLONNA *smiles and holds out his
hand. Handshake.* XAVIER *leaves.*
SOPHIE *emerges from the cupboard,
naked, wrapped in a blanket. Roaring
with laughter. She stops laughing
abruptly and shivers.*

SOPHIE. I'm cold warm me up

COLONNA. But it's quite hot in here

SOPHIE. I'm always cold

COLONNA *wraps her in two more
blankets, lifts her up and lays her on the
bed. Then he lies down beside her.*

Shall we make some tea? Piping hot
I think I love him

COLONNA. Yes

SOPHIE. You think so too?
At least *you* don't love me that's a
relief
And you're not wanting to marry me

COLONNA. I haven't exactly said I
don't love you

SOPHIE. It would be a relief if you did

COLONNA. China Tea? Ceylon?
Darjeeling?
You crying?

SOPHIE. I feel so miserable

COLONNA. You didn't answer
Darjeeling?

SOPHIE. Is that what you asked me?

COLONNA. Just now

SOPHIE. I don't know anything any
more
Oh I don't know what I want

COLONNA. And I made some
Darjeeling
My relationship with Mademoiselle
Auzanneau went on for three weeks
perhaps a month it was some time
before the tragedy I wonder what I'm
doing here I really didn't know her
well enough to be able to pass
judgement on her
The news was such a shock I may have
made certain remarks but I realise now
time has passed that they have little
bearing on the truth
For me she was a good companion
rather too intense at times it's been
said it was self-interest that made her
turn to me
Nothing could be further from the
truth
To be in my good books as her
examiner no truth in that at all I have
never been a member of any board of
examiners

CANCÉ. How did you feel then?

COLONNA. Feeling for her?

PRESIDENT. I must have order in the
Court

CANCÉ. About her

COLONNA. About her? An unlucky
sort of girl

PRESIDENT. I must ask the witness to
be good enough to wait until public
order is restored before proceeding
with his evidence

COLONNA. She chased after a love she
was never able to find it's undeniable
she was thrown off course by some of
the men who also chased after her and
indulged in blackmail to win her
consent that also helped to influence
her behaviour

CANCÉ. Thank you

PRESIDENT. Are there other witnesses
for the defence to call?
You were born?

SOPHIE. On March the 11th 1927 at
Dunkirk

PRESIDENT. Your father ran a plumbing and roofing business and your mother just kept house

In front of the Faculty of Medicine in Lille.

CLAUDETTE. Coming?

PRESIDENT. Though she helped to keep her husband's accounts

SOPHIE. Where?

CLAUDETTE. For a walk

SOPHIE. I'm in the dumps

PRESIDENT. You appear to have been your parents' favourite child yet you'll tell us you lacked affection Your father thought you were too brainy your mother didn't understand you is that correct?

CLAUDETTE. But you don't mind do you?

SOPHIE. He got through and I got a resit I won't put up with this separation I'm going to see him

CLAUDETTE. He's determined to go to Paris?

SOPHIE. I'll tell him I'm going with him

CLAUDETTE. Sure you know what you want to do?

CANCÉ. Sometimes up in your pear tree you took a book with you?

SOPHIE. I always kept a book in the pocket of my dungarees

CANCÉ. Do you remember any of the titles?

SOPHIE. *Gone with the wind*

PRESIDENT. Came our defeat and the ensuing Occupation it seems your father was not unduly affected by these events

CANCÉ. Romances? Novels?

SOPHIE. *Pride and Prejudice For whom the bell tolls*

PRESIDENT. In 1940 you were thirteen years old two of your three brothers were killed one on the submarine he commanded the other during an airforce exercise in 1941 when you were fourteen you were seen on the terrace of a café wearing a bathing costume in the company of German sailors

SOPHIE. *The sun also rises* usually American novels

PRESIDENT. And before you reached fifteen you went horse-riding with the Commander of the Occupation Forces one evening you go out for a walk arm in arm with a soldier of the Whermacht and you're stopped by a policeman who makes out a report the Headmistress of your school is stirred into action
Discreet measures were apparently taken which led to the defendant's expulsion after which she seems to have pursued her studies at home

CANCÉ. I have proof that this assertion is incorrect Monsieur le Président and I herewith submit the deposition of the Headmaster of the school not you notice the so-called Headmistress according to which Sophie Auzanneau was never excluded from his *lycée* during the Occupation
This is by no means the only example in this case of what would appear to be manipulation of the facts

PRESIDENT. I will not allow these proceedings to break the tradition of calm deliberation alone conducive to the pursuit of justice and the uncovering of the truth

On a pavement in Lille.

SOPHIE. Did you treat yourself to a new suit? It must be a must
When one's going to make one's first appearance in Paris
Turn around take a few steps it changes the way you walk
A bit loose round the shoulders

XAVIER. It was agony choosing it

SOPHIE. You should have taken me with you
Oh no that back's no good at all

XAVIER. What?

SOPHIE. The jacket doesn't hang straight

XAVIER. Sophie

SOPHIE. What?

XAVIER. You're doing this on purpose we were meant not to meet again

SOPHIE. Maybe I am maybe I've been too hard on you
I didn't know how I stood with you it took me time to find out
Now I know

XAVIER. Now it's too late

PRESIDENT. All your friends have said you were more annoyed than upset by this break-up

SOPHIE. Words I don't know what they mean

CANCÉ. Sophie Auzanneau fell in love with Xavier Bergeret at roughly the same moment as he stopped loving her

SOPHIE. I was in despair

LUBET. A black comedy of despair

CANCÉ. Since a man died I'd call it a tragedy

LUBET. A comedy at the first I repeat
A sinister comedy fabricated from start to finish out of pique
A carefully rehearsed performance inspired by blighted hope and by egocentric malice of the most savage and contemptible kind

SOPHIE. I'd like to try and say I'd like you to believe me

LUBET. In despair let's see what you did in your desperation
You went by train to Austria and as soon as you set foot in Vienna in great despair you find the real thing a love affair this time with a Monsieur Legouit a French engineer on assignment

SOPHIE. I'd like to try and explain
I'd always lived at home with my mother and father afraid to show my feelings
I never found it easy to talk about my personal problems to people who took no interest

PRESIDENT. But surely your mother would have noticed something

SOPHIE. Those who are closest to you sir may be the last ones to know you really well
In my home somehow we always lived cut off from one another you'd never imagine how cold my father was

LUBET. How I ask is this relevant to your idyllic Austrian romance?

SOPHIE. When I was small I thought he didn't love me at all so whether I felt happy or not I'd got into the habit of keeping it all to myself

SOPHIE's *room in Lille.*

CLAUDETTE. Why yes I promise you

SOPHIE. And he talked about me?
He hasn't forgotten me?

CLAUDETTE. Goodness I can hardly believe how you look
What a transformation

SOPHIE. Hang on I'll ask Madame Guibot to make us a cup of tea
What did he say Claudette tell me everything he said

PRESIDENT. In 1944 you were seventeen it was the end of the war the Allies had surrounded Dunkirk

CLAUDETTE. He was worried about you how things were going for you
And what you'd drifted into
He was hoping you hadn't been left on your own that there was someone to take care of you

PRESIDENT. The German authorities had all the civilians evacuated but you stayed on with your father

SOPHIE. No I had a room in the military hospital

CLAUDETTE. He was afraid you'd go to pieces

PRESIDENT. The hospital for the Wehrmacht

SOPHIE. He didn't say he'd like to well I don't know

CLAUDETTE. See you again? Oh no he said
It was over well and truly over he told me he'd got engaged to a girl called Francine
It seems to be a practical arrangement you know not a shattering affair
He'd had his share of grand passion he said
Settling down I guess

SOPHIE. Tell me his address

PRESIDENT. There you come across a
Colonel in the Medical Corps Doctor
Schlessinger a man of fifty-five you
were seventeen and you became his
mistress

CLAUDETTE. I don't know his address

SOPHIE. You're lying

CLAUDETTE. Perhaps you'll meet
again in a few years' time
You'll both have settled down and
you'll be swapping notes about the kids
you've each had
But now if you take my advice pack it
in

SOPHIE. You do know his address

CLAUDETTE. He usually confides in
me he's fond of me but I could tell he
was on his guard he knows I'm your closest
friend

SOPHIE. His address

PRESIDENT. The Allies' final onslaught
brought the conflict to an end

CLAUDETTE. Normally he would have
told me his address
We mustn't let our paths cross again

SOPHIE. He said that

PRESIDENT. But you are never to lose
sight of your Doctor the Colonel you
write to him and you go and see him
at Ulm in August 1950

LUBET. Only a few months before the
crime

SOPHIE. I've simply got to see him
Claudette

LUBET. A crime that's presented to us
as a crime of passion

CLAUDETTE. It's a bit late to wake up
to him now

LUBET. What did she want from him?
Money no doubt

SOPHIE. I didn't realise

LUBET. It's all one to Sophie
Auzanneau which lover she pursues

SOPHIE. Can you lend me two thousand
francs?

LUBET. Young or old German or French

SOPHIE. For the train fare

I'll pay you back in a week I'm going
to my parents for my birthday there's
an envelope waiting for me with some
cash

LUBET. She never returned the loan of
course

CLAUDETTE. I'm sure she would if
events had turned out differently

SOPHIE. Let me have the two thousand
francs

CLAUDETTE. Now you've got this
other bloke after what you tell me he's
a decent sort he's got a good position
and he wants what's best for you
Go and live abroad for a while
Vienna's a lovely city
What's his name?

SOPHIE. Legouit
Just now I can't think about Legouit

CLAUDETTE. He's in love with you
and you say you love him
Turn the page

SOPHIE. I get my pages mixed up
I need that address

CLAUDETTE. You never stopped
telling him you weren't the wife for
him
You made him believe it in the end

SOPHIE. On my knees I'll go on my
knees to him
Oh Claudette today I'm ready to agree
to anything
I'll be the wife he's dreamed of

PRESIDENT. You arrived at the Gare
du Nord
Then what did you do?

SOPHIE. I went straight to his place

PRESIDENT. You hadn't seen him for

SOPHIE. Eighteen months

LUBET. I note Monsieur le Président
that the defendant contradicts herself
in a previous statement she made it
clear it was not until the morning of
the following day that she charged in
on Bergeret having spent the night at a
hotel

SOPHIE. I hadn't the money for a hotel
room
I went straight to his place

PRESIDENT. And then what?

SOPHIE. He let me in

PRESIDENT. What happened next?

SOPHIE. We had supper

PRESIDENT. In his room?

SOPHIE. Yes

PUBLIC PROSECUTOR. The events
leading up to this bloodbath have now
been pieced together
It was all worked out in advance down
to the smallest detail the admissions
made at this hearing?
All calculated
A bloodbath and a torrent of lies
There may be talk of other affairs but
I tell you no affair is quite like any
other and Members of the Jury you
weren't party to them anyway so let us
stick to our affair and ignore all the
rest

The hospital in Dunkirk. SOPHIE *is
wearing a white coat.*

DR SCHLESSINGER. What is there to
eat?

SOPHIE. You look tired

DR SCHLESSINGER. You're my one
consolation
Today they arrived in droves badly
wounded

SOPHIE. Young Wolfgang died spitting
blood
I held his hand

DR SCHLESSINGER. There should be
more little French girls warm-hearted
like you
Now you can come and hop on my lap
So I can give my little kitten a cuddle

SOPHIE. Gently now
You're going to lose this war

DR SCHLESSINGER. Never

SOPHIE. And I shall lose you
Will you take me with you?

DR SCHLESSINGER. What would Frau
Schlessinger say?

PUBLIC PROSECUTOR. I oppose and
reject any plea for diminished
responsibility or extenuating
circumstances our distinguished experts
have made much of her temperamental
character but I tell you these experts
have misread the motive
Sophie was hell-bent on destroying any
chance of happiness because Sophie is
a monster
Wasn't she a monster already as an
adolescent when she linked up with our
invaders?
Between them and her there was a
great affinity
And isn't she still a monster when the
day before her trial is due to start in
the very last moments before her
feigned attempt at suicide she makes
out a will in favour of who you may
ask? In the name of a woman
sentenced to hard labour for life
A woman who had killed her first child
aged eighteen months and five years
later a second one and in both cases
claimed that their death was accidental
Once again Sophie Auzanneau found a
great affinity with this odious woman
Not without reason did Xavier
Bergeret say she was devastating
So this death that she brought upon
him

XAVIER's *room in Paris.*

XAVIER. God
What are you doing here?

PUBLIC PROSECUTOR. I now call
down upon her

SOPHIE. Can I sit down?

XAVIER. Sit

PUBLIC PROSECUTOR. Not in the
smallest measure

SOPHIE. It's nice for you here

XAVIER. Think so?

SOPHIE. It's cheerful like you

PUBLIC PROSECUTOR. Can I find it
in my heart to forgive her
In defence of humanity and our feeble
hopes of happiness I demand for this
monster the ultimate penalty

CANCÉ. I stand up alone
To face these extravagant allegations
For this is all wild exaggeration and
the very enormity of it weighs me
down like a cloak of lead

SOPHIE. Have you got a bathroom too?

XAVIER. See for yourself

SOPHIE. All you need eh you haven't changed

XAVIER. Nor you

SOPHIE. I have

XAVIER. Still got your cat?

SOPHIE. Madame Guibot looks after her
You don't hear too much noise from the traffic is this new?

XAVIER. This kit
A friend in electronics put it together for me

SOPHIE. Do you listen to lots of music?
Do you still believe there are only three or four possible situations?

XAVIER. With variations

SOPHIE. Did you learn in the end
How to do your own ironing?
Can I take my shoes off?

XAVIER. Where have you come from?

SOPHIE. Gare du Nord

XAVIER. Who gave you the address?

SOPHIE. Are you cross?

XAVIER. No
It's just that we agreed

SOPHIE. I know
You want me to go?

XAVIER. You've taken your shoes off
So stay for a while

SOPHIE. Can I invite you to supper?

XAVIER. I'm inviting you there's left-overs in the fridge

LUBET. Lies lies lies a barrage of lies

PRESIDENT. If you don't mind Maître I have not yet finished the cross-examination

LUBET. On the morning of the 7th of March she took Xavier by surprise at No. 25 rue de l'Abbé Groult
The address she'd wrung out of her friend as we heard
Some minutes later she left having realised the break was beyond repair
As she went out she made the following remark 'if that's the way it is all I can do now is disappear'
We know because next day Xavier repeated it word for word to his

fiancée Francine
These Monsieur le Président are the facts

PRESIDENT. For Heaven's sake Maître let us take things one at a time
You took a room in a hotel

SOPHIE. I took the métro at the Gare du Nord and went straight to his place
We had supper in his room

PRESIDENT. What did you talk about?

SOPHIE. Nothing of importance

PRESIDENT. You hadn't seen him for eighteen months you say you were madly in love with him and you spoke of nothing of importance?

SOPHIE. Yes but we spent the night together

PRESIDENT. I will have order in this Court

LUBET. So when you were asked by the police why didn't you mention this before?

SOPHIE. I didn't want to tell anyone about it
I just said he'd kissed me the way he used to

PUBLIC PROSECUTOR. I rather think you kept quiet about it because you weren't sure that Bergeret was dead and you felt he might have denied it
Only when you found you really had killed him did it occur to you to fabricate a story to make it look more like a crime of passion
So this night you spent together is pure invention

CANCÉ. Who is inventing making up stories now?
Public Prosecutor sir you reduce me to despair your legal procedure is so finely tuned in such good working order that it would leave me defenceless were it not for my open mind my probity
So I am uneasy
In the course of my professional career I have tried to come to terms with the clients I defend get to like them for what they are try and understand them
And you Members of the Jury should make an effort to understand too
By looking closely into yourselves at your own faults your own misgivings

And if it so happens you can find none
Then by considering the failings and
misfortunes of others

PRESIDENT. And you returned to
Lille?

SOPHIE. Yes the day after

PRESIDENT. This time it is Madame
Guibot your landlady's evidence which
enlightens us
Madame Guibot was more than a
landlady to you
Someone you could confide in? Not
unlike an accomplice?

Mme GUIBOT. Me an accomplice sir?

PRESIDENT. Don't misunderstand me I
know you sent that telegram and
warned the boy's father by telephone
you did the right and proper thing
But you felt some sympathy for your
tenant a sort of indulgence almost
motherly
You understood her as it seems her
own mother had never done

DR SCHLESSINGER's *surgery at Ulm.*

DR SCHLESSINGER. What an
absolutely wonderful surprise
My little ray of sunshine

SOPHIE. My cavalier my first one

DR SCHLESSINGER. Problems?

SOPHIE? Bernd
I simply had to see you

DR SCHLESSINGER. Some special
reason?

SOPHIE. I miss you terribly
Every single day

DR SCHLESSINGER. I'm an old quack
an old Boche unappetising at that
And you're a splendid young woman
of twenty-three
My kitten's grown into a tigress

SOPHIE. Don't joke about it
If the world was a better place
We'd be living together

DR SCHLESSINGER. Recognise this
pebble?

SOPHIE. The Doctor still keeps it in his
pocket?

DR SCHLESSINGER. Now you're a

doctor too?

SOPHIE. No

DR SCHLESSINGER. Married?

SOPHIE. No

DR SCHLESSINGER. What about that
boy who wanted to marry you and you
wouldn't

SOPHIE. Now he doesn't want to and I
do

DR SCHLESSINGER. So the world is a
pretty awful place
Let's change it

SOPHIE. We'll rub it out and start again

DR SCHLESSINGER. Where have you
just come from? Lille? Paris?

SOPHIE. I'm living in Vienna with a
very nice man who says he never fell
for anyone like me before
Bernd I want to stay here with you for
a day or two

DR SCHLESSINGER. That won't be
too easy with Frau Schlessinger around

SOPHIE. I don't mind a hotel if I can
see you for an hour every day
You've nothing to fear from me Bernd
I'm not wicked or mad
It's just that I must

DR SCHLESSINGER. And your
Viennese gentleman?

SOPHIE. Do you know Vienna Bernd?
A gingerbread city a long way from
the sea
A part of it's subsiding and my
gentleman's got the job of
underpinning it
He wants us to get married I told him
I needed a few days away to think it
over

DR SCHLESSINGER. You haven't
learnt much

SOPHIE. I don't know anything Bernd
any more

DR SCHLESSINGER. My tigress can't
decide which way to jump next

SOPHIE. Any nice forests round here?

DR SCHLESSINGER. I've heard tales
of woods in Vienna

SOPHIE. Not even a tree just one tree?

PRESIDENT. Right in front of him

Why did you throw yourself under his very eyes into the arms of Monsieur Colonna a man you didn't love?
To taunt him? Or just out of cruelty?

SOPHIE. Can you know in advance if love will come?

PRESIDENT. Xavier knew he was in love with you but you didn't love him you told us yourself what you felt for him was not love but affection so why keep him on the hook for so long?

SOPHIE. It's true my feelings weren't the same as his I thought at the time we couldn't ever be happy together
At least I didn't realise we could
But then I came to see I was really in love

PRESIDENT. All the more surprising then if you were so fond of him
All the more surprising that you should get involved with this engineer this Monsieur Legouit in Austria who you then walked out on to go and spend a few days at Ulm with your former lover Doctor Schlessinger
One can't help wondering who you're in love with
A little order Ladies and Gentlemen in this courtroom

SOPHIE. If there was no hope for me with Bergeret I had to get fixed up with someone else I'd got it wrong once already
It had made me very unhappy I didn't want to make another mistake I wasn't sure I was in love with Legouit

PRESIDENT. That is not the impression one gets when reading your letters to him let me quote from one
'This is the first time making some man happy or seeing that he's happy for some other reason
Has meant more to me
Than my own self-gratification'

SOPHIE. I never realised
Anyway it didn't stop me thinking about Bergeret

PUBLIC PROSECUTOR. Didn't you say that with patience your fidelity would bring Bergeret round?
One can't help wondering what you understand by fidelity

SOPHIE. It's hard to explain

PRESIDENT. Laughter in this court is

out of place

Mme GUIBOT. And then I put my hand in her bag and pulled out the bottle that contained the fatal concoction
Your young gentleman's all of a piece I told her he's straight as they come
He was in love with you you put him off so he broke it off

PRESIDENT. A good summing-up

Mme GUIBOT. And I pointed out there were other fish to fry
She knew there were others all right
That all happened a fortnight after they broke up and he moved to Paris he came back to Lille for a day or two she found out and wanted to talk to him he agreed to meet her but he refused to take up with her again and she threatened to poison herself Monsieur Xavier got into a state and came in to warn me I rushed upstairs fast as I could with my rheumatics.

SOPHIE's room in Lille.

Where's your handbag?

SOPHIE. Here

Mme GUIBOT. What is it?

SOPHIE. Cyanide

Mme GUIBOT. Better have a good cry than swallow this muck

SOPHIE. They say it's got a nasty taste
I've no choice it's all too much for me
there's no way out leave me alone

Mme GUIBOT. I don't remember what I said next but her tears started so I stroked her hair and she fell asleep with her head on my shoulder

LUBET. Obviously a put-up job a sly bit of blackmail

CANCÉ. That no one should remain in ignorance
When Monsieur Auzanneau heard what his daughter had done he took his own life he was found with a gas pipe in his mouth his body full of ether
Earlier on he had sent Monsieur Bergeret a letter of excuse and condolence

SOPHIE. In my family no one ever seems to die a natural death

PRESIDENT. You can judge for yourselves how genuine were her attempts at suicide
May I recall the report drawn up by Doctor Paul following the attempt which forced us into an adjournment Sophie Auzanneau made good use of her medical knowledge first she applied a tourniquet to her left forearm then with a needle or a piece of broken glass we're not quite sure which she cut clean into the radial vein
She lost about a litre of blood and was found comatose in her cell at six o'clock this morning when I saw her at ten she was still in the same condition Pulse rate impossible to count blood pressure under six
But next morning she had recovered enough of her strength and her mental faculties to compose a letter she addressed to me which reads as follows
'I am obliged to write this letter in the dark as I don't want to switch the night light on
I hope Monsieur and Madame Bergeret will forgive me if they can and take pity on my mother I'm sorry for all I've done
I bitterly regret that I killed him
But I will not submit to a system of justice devoid of all dignity I refuse to be tried in public in front of a crowd that reminds me of the howling mobs of the Revolution my trial ought to have been held *in camera* I'm glad I've been able to thwart the officials who set the stage for this masquerade'
I shall not ask you Sophie Auzanneau whether you have had second thoughts about this scurrilous attack on the law

PUBLIC PROSECUTOR. To slow the Law down that above all was your strategy Sophie Auzanneau to drag it all out
Thanks to your squalid performance you have gained seven weeks

CANCÉ. I object to this interpretation from the representative of the State I too have received a letter from my client
A heart-rending one
Which with your permission I shall not make public

PRESIDENT. In the moments that followed the crime because we have to return to that
Did you Sophie Auzanneau really intend to put an end to your life?
Or was it rather
To use your own words?
An attempt to set the stage?
Would our expert like to throw some light on this point?

DR HAUDEBOURG. For Sophie Auzanneau there seems to be something normal and logical about suicide she was brought up to think like this
In our psychiatric report we specifically referred to it as a theatrical suicide and yes we chose the expression with care
We called it theatrical to draw attention to its flamboyance and not to say it was simulated

The bed in XAVIER'*s room in Lille.*

SOPHIE. Xavier

XAVIER. Yes

SOPHIE. I feel sleepy

XAVIER. Relax with my arms round you

SOPHIE. In your arms yes
And not wake up again
Why is everything so difficult?
Why does it hurt so?
Why do I hurt you so much?
How long is this going to last?

LUBET. I'm not going to muddy the issue
When a spade is a spade
I'm outspoken enough to say so
The defence is engaged in a subtle manoeuvre designed to trap you into understanding while at the same time befogging you in clouds of mystification

XAVIER. You're all snuggled up but you're tensed up too
How can you
If only you could let yourself go

SOPHIE. Let myself go
Yes
If you knew how I'd like to
But then you know I can't
I can't

LUBET. The defence prefers to dwell in that somewhat disturbing twilight zone

where the line dividing what is from
what is not becomes blurred

SOPHIE. Can you hear
The storm
About to cause havoc in the garden
Papa had to get up in the middle of the
night
I'm afraid

XAVIER. Afraid of what? I'm here

SOPHIE. Of myself
Of everything
I should never have told you about the
sardines
The trunk splits and the branch gets
broken
My cat has slipped under the netting
Gone a-roving
Do you love me? And do I love you?
Words that don't come neat in their
little compartments
But go rolling rolling on

LUBET. Understanding what escapes all
understanding of course so you are no
longer able to pass judgement
Because judgement ah Members of the
Jury judgement

SOPHIE. Like a pebble
You ought to break me open to find
out what's inside

LUBET. Judgement as André Malraux
said is clearly the negation of
understanding
Never mind if I break the spell and
drag you back to earth
There one can understand and pass
judgement in the full light of day

SOPHIE. Break me with your teeth
Bite me
Hard
Where am I? Who is it?

XAVIER. It's me
And it's you
Here

SOPHIE. Where?
One day you know I'll kill you
To simplify

XAVIER. What will that simplify?

SOPHIE. Do you know why you love
me?

XAVIER. I know how it all began
I loved your laugh before I loved your
face

In the large lecture-room I could
sometimes hear this laugh coming from
a bench behind me

SOPHIE. When did you find out which
face it belonged to?

XAVIER. One day I followed a girl out
of the lecture-room she was beautiful
and on the boulevard between two
rows of plane trees she said to me
chance and fate are two sides of the
same coin
It stuck in my mind you see because
then she laughed and I recognised the
laugh I'd heard behind me
A laugh that has nothing to do with a
sense of humour

SOPHIE. She doesn't have a sense of
humour?

XAVIER. None at all

SOPHIE. So she can't enjoy a joke
What if the whole of her life was a
joke?

XAVIER. She blew hot and cold
Is that what I loved about her?

SOPHIE. Look
It's going to be fine today
It'll be the most beautiful day
To learn how to love loving perhaps
I hope one can learn how I do so want
To be able to love

LUBET. You don't need to make up
your minds about whether a crime was
committed or who the guilty party is
the admissions already made by the
defendant have relieved us of this
obligation
You only have to resolve two problems
premeditation and mitigating
circumstances and your response will
depend upon the personal conviction
you have each of you formed
concerning the motives for the crime
What the defence puts forward is
woolly and obscure
Attempting to lead you astray
Whereas I shall demonstrate

XAVIER. That's what I like you're the
one I want

SOPHIE. But I hurt you

XAVIER. The first night you spent with
me
You said I was hurting you

LUBET. I shall prove that the one and only motive for the crime was self-interest

At the Auzanneaus' house in Lille.

M. AUZANNEAU. You're not going to like this much
Though with you one can never tell
Henri is dead

SOPHIE. I'm often like that
Henri who?

M. AUZANNEAU. Your brother

Mme AUZANNEAU. She was always at loggerheads with her elder brother

M. AUZANNEAU. His submarine has been sunk

Mme AUZANNEAU. With the other one it wasn't the same
She seems to have grieved for him

M. AUZANNEAU. She showed nothing

SOPHIE's room in Lille.

CLAUDETTE. Why?

SOPHIE. Yes why do you think he wanted to know who was sleeping with me?

CLAUDETTE. His affair with you may be at an end but that doesn't stop him you know still taking an interest in you

Mme AUZANNEAU. Our little girl was precocious emotionally

M. AUZANNEAU. The war didn't help

SOPHIE. Did you feel he was jealous?

CLAUDETTE. Of course a touch of jealousy it's a natural reaction
Anyone would think it's good news I'm bringing you
But Sophie no he won't see you any more he's getting married it's over

LUBET. Self-interest
The crime of an opportunist a money-grubbing woman set on marriage
Whose interest in men is stimulated only by their status
A fortune-hunter
If she got Xavier in her clutches it's because Xavier was the most desirable and if she left him later it's because he wouldn't have her any more
The men she tried to seduce after that also appealed to her only because of their money or their position Colonna Legouit
She discovers that the first man is not the marrying type and the business prospects of the second didn't equal her expectations
Then she wants to go back to Xavier Bergeret
But the young man is unshakeable he has made up his mind he gets engaged to Francine no hope left there
So she reached her decision
Every avenue is closed to her and she will not allow this man to seize his chance of happiness
She will shoot him down
With a revolver in her pocket she waits for him in the entrance to his block of flats
Like a killer
Is this your drama of love?
She has thought it all out
She fires the first bullet into his back he collapses she walks all round the body
Fires a second time at his forehead
Then the *coup de grâce* at zero range into his temple
Of course it's only a hypothesis

PUBLIC PROSECUTOR. On a café terrace in her bathing costume in the company of German sailors.

A café terrace in Paris.

CORNAILLE. Don't let her in

XAVIER. You mustn't all drop her completely or she'll just let herself drift

Mme GUIBOT. I wouldn't say I'd had a premonition but I'd use a cup of tea as an excuse
At odd times I'd go upstairs and suggest a cup of tea
On her bed I saw a will a paper anyway and on it she'd written will

CORNAILLE. He was an honest frank straightforward fellow incapable of deception

LACHAUD. A gentleman that's the

word from a united family his father
was a vet at Saint-Omer

Mme GUIBOT. She must have tiptoed
down the stairs I never heard her come
down
She'd been lying up there all depressed
for a couple of days and then suddenly
no one there not even her shopping-
bag

CLAUDETTE. It was as if something
had made her happy
Yes at that moment there was a change
in her character

Mme GUIBOT. I sent my telegram off

CLAUDETTE. She didn't seem so
strange to me not so hard
I was much more drawn to her

Mme GUIBOT. The telephone call to his
father too
To Saint-Omer where he had his clinic

CORNAILLE. He loved her ''tis pity
she's a whore' he said to me one day
but that remark should be taken sir as
typical of a student for us
It didn't have the same literal meaning
a policeman would give it

LACHAUD. Though he really had
grown away from her there was a
lingering trace of compassion

PRESIDENT. Your past life is what one
might call erratic tempestuous even

Mme GUIBOT. I used to do her washing
for her
One morning when I took her clean
clothes back there she was starkers in
bed she always used to sleep in her
birthday suit even in the winter with
ten below freezing outside
Someone came in without knocking it
was Monsieur Xavier he slipped into
bed beside her fully dressed the two of
them never took no notice of me
She asked me if I'd bring up two cups
of tea

PUBLIC PROSECUTOR. So now we
can trace in ghastly clarity the
emergence of this blackguardly scheme
in which every step was calculated
She didn't take the lift
She climbed the stairs from one floor
to the next with a brief pause perhaps
on each landing
In order to rehearse every move she

was about to make
With him unbeknowing upstairs
And her
With her foot in the door in case he
should reject her once more
It's terrifying
At least let us not be afraid to call
things by their proper name this is the
unscrupulous perfidy of a woman who
had worked everything out weighed up
all the pros and cons

CORNAILLE. He had warned me never
to give her his address

LACHAUD. We were on our guard

CORNAILLE. We knew she was proud
intelligent romantic

LACHAUD. But we never thought her
capable of this

DR SCHLESSINGER's surgery at Ulm.

SOPHIE. I feel tired Bernd

DR SCHLESSINGER. I told Frau
Schlessinger I had to perform an
operation this evening
Till late at night

SOPHIE. Say something nice to me

CORNAILLE. Xavier was a great guy
and Sophie Auzanneau wasn't the kind
of girl a fellow like him could take as a
wife

DR SCHLESSINGER. In the hospital at
Dunkirk there was a little parrot do
you remember?

SOPHIE. My cat used to prowl around
him ferociously While the bombs were
dropping

LACHAUD. Sophie Auzanneau wasn't
good enough for Xavier
Xavier reproached her with what we all
blamed her for betraying him making a
fool of him over Colonna and the rest
All she ever wanted was to do her own
thing

SOPHIE. Maybe in my whole life I've
never been happier

SOPHIE's room in Lille.

XAVIER. Just over a year ago I asked

you to be my wife
In spite of all that's happened I'm
asking you again today

FRANCINE. He told me at once that
he'd known this woman but it was over
Since he first got to know me I'm sure
absolutely positive he hasn't seen her
again

LACHAUD. It's true I never had much
sympathy for her myself

PRESIDENT. So I'd like to ask you
whether in your concern for justice this
feeling of repulsion for her has been
moderated?

SOPHIE. No Xavier don't ask me that

XAVIER. Is this your last word?

LACHAUD. Did I mention repulsion?
In any case I'm sure even Xavier
Wouldn't approve of all this

With a slight gesture around him

PUBLIC PROSECUTOR. Wouldn't
approve of all this? Aha
But he must have foreseen it all and
that must be right if I'm to believe
your own evidence for that telegram
was passed on to you with the words
May I ask you to repeat them?

LACHAUD. 'If anything happens to me'

PUBLIC PROSECUTOR. And in fact
didn't something happen to him?
Something premeditated

LUBET. The life of this young man

PUBLIC PROSECUTOR. Can there be
any doubt about it?

LUBET. Like all those who are really
strong he was honest and upright
The happiness of that united family yes
who had everything going for them
Has all been swept away destroyed
annihilated by Sophie Auzanneau's
criminal act
Death broken lives indescribable
suffering and it's all due to you Sophie
Auzanneau though you seem hardly
aware of it
Obsessed as you are with yourself
Hour after hour month after month
we've been hanging on your lips for
one word of regret or excuse hoping
for a hint of repentance in your eyes
But your mouth has been silent your
eyes have shown nothing but the glint

of a hard heart
So don't expect either pardon or mercy
from us

SOPHIE. You'd laugh at my landlady
Bernd she watches over me with a
gruff kindness I never knew at home
She does my washing for me and brings
me tea

DR SCHLESSINGER. You let it get
cold you always have you always say
you like it piping hot
Then you leave it for hours to get cold

At the Auzanneaus' house at Dunkirk.

Mme AUZANNEAU. She's twenty-four
an age when one should think about
marriage it's time she settled down
A postcard from her she's all right and
she'll be here as usual for her birthday

SOPHIE. She loves telling me off when
are you going to stop chasing around
like an Amazon?
She's convinced the Amazons are
natives a tribe of wild women who are
cannibals in South America

M. AUZANNEAU. We spent enough on
her education didn't we?

SOPHIE. Yet at the same time I get the
feeling she'd protect me if anyone tried
to hurt me

Mme AUZANNEAU. We did all we
could the same as we would for the
others

CANCÉ. But there you have it she'd
been told never to show her feelings in
her face she was taught to distrust
people's faces

DR SCHLESSINGER. I never met a girl
I fancied as much as you

SOPHIE. Shut up Bernd

DR SCHLESSINGER. No let me tell
you
I've a fancy to give up my practice and
carry this girl off to a place where we
could go native she'd hunt for game
and I'd roast it
Somewhere far away near the Amazon

M. AUZANNEAU. It's like we never
existed except to cough up when she
comes collecting for her birthday

Mme AUZANNEAU. Aren't they all like that these days?

M. AUZANNEAU. Never a word of thanks no gratitude

CANCÉ. Monstrous
The influence of a family whose chief aim was to come out on top
Choke any sign of affection and then you can savour your success such was the appalling upbringing yes monstrous the Prosecutor found the right word inflicted on this girl who was encouraged to be proud and arrogant
A murderess yes Members of the Jury but a victim as well a victim not a torturer unless it be to torture herself
The psychiatrists who were rather hastily discounted by the Prosecutor are may I remind you experts you chose for yourself
If you made a bad choice why don't you dismiss them? You usually have faith in them don't you? It just seems
That in this case you ignore anything you find embarrassing
You ignore everything that might tend to demolish your theory of premeditation
A highly improbable theory but gifted as we know you are you make up for your failure to prove it by pursuing it with a ruthlessness which in all my career I have rarely witnessed before
One of the three shots fired was at zero range and you thought fit to label it the *coup de grâce* the death-blow it's so easy to say but
How was it fired? Suddenly as his body crumpled it must have fallen against her and set the revolver off and this turns out to be your *coup de grâce* a set of facts can be interpreted in any way you like

CLAUDETTE. There are so many crossed lines Monsieur le Président
I'm not sure that there wasn't a time when he was still in love with her and she had started to love him
We all went to Antwerp once the three of us together to visit a museum

CANCÉ. If after the attempt to take her life last month my client was able to write 'I believe there's a curse on my family and on me as well' if she was able to understand that the time had come to make a confession

The Fine Art Museum in Antwerp.

SOPHIE. Look at that character

XAVIER. Which one?

SOPHIE. Leaning out of the window the sporty-looking type with something on his mind up there in the right-hand corner I like that picture
He looks like you

XAVIER. And the girl with the red scarf on the other side of the road who seems to be gazing at him she looks like you

CANCÉ. If she was able to write 'I hope Monsieur and Madame Bergeret can forgive me and take pity on my mother' doesn't this suggest she realised the time had come for her to redeem herself? So on her behalf
And with her own words
I ask you to forgive a girl whose real sin was pride

SOPHIE. She's horrible

XAVIER. I think she's not bad

SOPHIE. Are you serious?

XAVIER. If I met her in the street

SOPHIE. With that green nose and her yellow hands
I never realised

XAVIER. I'd follow her

SOPHIE. And I'd go for the sporty young raver with something on his mind I don't think the girl has treated him all that well look you can see she's going to eat her heart out

CANCÉ. And I believe I can ask you to forgive all those parents who think they know how to bring up their children and who make them into a replica of themselves living cheek by jowl with them without learning to know them at all I ask you to forgive the manner in which she defended herself and the blunders she made

SOPHIE. I wonder if the painter let the red paint run down the canvas on purpose
It looks as if her heart's been bleeding I never realised

CANCÉ. Forgive her too for having chosen to defend her
A feeble servant of the law

Who if he refuses to give way to tears
can only appeal to you with all the
dignity he can muster

CLAUDETTE. You're taking your time

SOPHIE. Come and see and tell us if
you think
If those two got together
It could lead to anything?

CLAUDETTE. It's an enormous picture

SOPHIE. Who painted it?

XAVIER. James Ensor

RECORDED VOICE. Sentences Sophie
Auzanneau to penal servitude for life

STRUGGLE OF THE DOGS AND THE BLACK

Translated by Matthew Ward

BERNARD-MARIE KOLTÈS began by writing plays for the theatre students at the Strasbourg National Drama School. Since the publication in 1980 of *Night just before the Forest* (a dramatic monologue) and *Struggle of the Dogs and the Black*, he has had two more plays published by Éditions de Minuit: *Quai Ouest (Western Dock)* and *Dans la solitude des champs de coton (In the Loneliness of the Cotton Fields)*. He has built up a close working relationship with Patrice Chéreau's Théâtre des Amandiers at Nanterre, where his adaptation of *A Winter's Tale* was staged in 1987. *Struggle of the Dogs and the Black* – a rich tragedy of neo-colonialist conflict – was premièred in a lavish production by Patrice Chéreau (1984); the play has a cast of only four and has been equally successful in small-budget productions.

Characters

The first production of *Struggle of the Dogs and the Black* (then entitled *Come Dog, Come Night*) was given in Matthew Ward's English translation by Ubu Repertory Theater at La Mama in New York on December 9, 1982 with the following cast:

HORN	Louis Zorich
ALBOURY	Afemo
LEONA	Barbara eda-Young
CAL	Ron Frazier

Directed by Françoise Kourilsky
Designed by Roberto Moscoso
Lighting by Beverly Emmons
Music by Aiyb Dieng and Teko Manong

HORN, *sixty years old; foreman of project*
ALBOURY, *a black who has mysteriously gained entry into the camp*
LEONA, *a woman brought by* HORN
CAL, *in his thirties; an engineer*

'He called the child born to him in exile Nouofia, which means "conceived in the desert".'

Alboury: king of the Douiloff (Ouoloff), in the nineteenth century, who opposed the white incursion.

Toubab: common name for whites in certain regions of Africa.

'The jackal pounces on an abandoned carcass, greedily tears off a few mouthfuls, eats on the run; uncatchable and unrepentant scavenger, sometime killer.'

'Along both coasts of the Cape, it was certain death, and in the middle, a mountain of ice, to which the blind who ran into it would be condemned.'

'Throughout the long suffocation of her victim, in a meditative and ritual ecstasy, obscurely, the lioness remembers the possessions of love.'

SCENE

In a West African country, anywhere from Senegal to Nigeria, a construction site for a public works project of a foreign company.

The CAMP:

encircled by high fences and observation towers, where the supervisory personnel live and building materials are stored:

- a large clump of bougainvillea; a van is pulled up under a tree;
- a veranda, table and rocking chairs, a bottle of whiskey;
- the door of one of the bungalows half open

The CONSTRUCTION SITE:

a river runs through it; an uncompleted bridge; in the distance, a lake.

THE CALLS OF THE GUARD:

Sounds of tongues and throats, of iron striking iron, iron striking wood, faint cries, gasps, whistling, brief chants, which stream over the barbed wire like a barrage of laughter or a coded message, blocking out the sounds of the bush surrounding the camp.

THE BRIDGE:

Two symmetrical constructions, gigantic and white, of concrete and cables, which rise up out of the red sand, but do not meet, in a huge and empty sky, above a river of mud.

Ouleff translations by Alioune Badara Fall.

Scene One

Behind the bougainvillaea, at twilight.

HORN. I was sure I saw somebody, over there, behind that tree.

ALBOURY. I am Alboury, sir. I have come for the body. His mother came to the workyard to lay branches on the body, but she found nothing, nothing at all. And she will wander about the village, wailing, all night long, if she is not given the body. A terrible night, sir, no one will be able to sleep for the old woman's cries. That is why I have come.

HORN. Was it the police, Mr Alboury, or the village that sent you?

ALBOURY. I am Alboury, sir, I have come in search of my brother's body.

HORN. A terrible situation, yes; a bad fall. An unfortunate accident; a truck came speeding through. The driver will be punished. The workers are reckless, despite the strict instructions they're given. You'll get the body, tomorrow. They must have taken it to the infirmary, to fix it up a little, for a proper presentation to the family. Please give them my condolences. And my condolences to you too. Such a sad situation!

ALBOURY. Sad, yes. Sad, no. If he had not been a worker, sir, the family would have buried the empty gourd in the earth and said, 'One less mouth to feed'. All the same, it's one less mouth to feed since the project is soon to close and, in a short time, he would no longer have been a worker, so it soon would have been one more mouth to feed. So it is only sad for a little while, sir.

HORN. But you, I've never seen you around here before. Come have a little whisky. Don't stand there behind that tree, I can hardly see you. Come and sit down at the table with me. Here, on this project, we have excellent relations with the police and the local authorities. I pride myself on that.

ALBOURY. The village has talked of you ever since work began. So I said, 'Here is my chance to see the white up close'. For I still have many things to learn, sir, and I said to my soul, 'Run to my ears and listen, run to my eyes and remember all that you see'.

HORN. In any case you express yourself remarkably well in French, and in English and other languages too, probably. You all have a remarkable gift for languages. Are you an official of some kind? You have a certain class about you, like an official. And you know more than you let on. Well now, that's quite a string of compliments.

ALBOURY. A useful way to begin.

HORN. It's strange. In most cases the village sends us a delegation and things are taken care of pretty fast. Things are usually done more formally, but fast. Eight or ten people, eight or ten of the dead man's brothers . . . I'm used to making fast deals. Sad about your brother, you call everybody 'brother' here, don't you? I know the family wants some sort of compensation. They'll get it, of course, whoever it's due to, if they don't go overboard. But you, though, I'm sure I've never seen you before.

ALBOURY. I have come only for the body, sir, and I will leave as soon as I get it.

HORN. Yeah, yeah, yeah, the body! You'll get it tomorrow. I'm sorry I'm so nervous. I have a lot on my mind. My wife's just arrived. She's been unpacking and arranging her things for hours. I don't know what she thinks of the place. Having a woman here is a big change, I'm not used to it.

ALBOURY. It is very good to have a woman here.

HORN. I was just recently married, very, very recently. In fact, I can tell you, it hasn't even been finalized yet, I mean the formalities. But getting married is a big change in any case. I'm not at all used to this sort of thing. It's causing me a lot of worry and her not coming out of her room makes me nervous. She just stays inside there, arranging her things, for hours now. Let's have a drink while we wait for her, I'll introduce her to you, we'll have a little celebration, and you can stay. But come over to the table now, there's hardly any light left here. My eyes aren't what they used to be. Come on now, let's have a look at you.

ALBOURY. Impossible, sir. Look at the guards, look at them, up there. They are watching inside the camp as well as outside. I am the one they watch. If they see me sit down with you, they will be suspicious of me. They say, 'Do not trust the goat that lives in the lion's den.' Do not be offended by what they say. To be a lion is clearly more honourable than to be a goat.

HORN. But they let you in. You generally need a pass or you have to be an official representative of some sort. They know that.

ALBOURY. They know that the old woman cannot be left to cry through the night and tomorrow too, that she must be calmed, that the village cannot be left without sleep, and that the mother must be satisfied by the body's return. They know very well why I have come.

HORN. We'll have it taken out to you tomorrow. Meantime, my head's about to split, I need a drink. It's a crazy thing for an old man like me to have brought a woman here, isn't it?

ALBOURY. Women are not crazy things. Besides, they say, 'The best soup comes from old pots.' Do not be offended by what they say Women have their way of saying things, but it is very honourable for you.

HORN. Even getting married?

ALBOURY. Especially getting married. First you must pay them their price, and keep a tight hold on them after.

HORN. You're a smart man, Mr Alboury. I think she's coming out. Come on, come on, let's have a chat. The glasses are already out. You can't stay behind that tree, in the dark. Why don't you join me?

ALBOURY. I cannot. My eyes cannot take such bright light. They blink and burn. They are not used to the strong lights you use at night.

HORN. Come on, come on, you'll be able to see her.

ALBOURY. I will see her from a distance.

HORN. My head is splitting, mister. What could she be doing all this time? I want to ask her what she thinks of the place. Do you know the surprise? I've got so much on my mind! I'm putting on a fireworks display, tonight – stay for it. I must be out of my mind, it cost me a fortune. And then we'll discuss this other business. Yes, we've always had excellent relations with the authorities. I've got them in the palm of my hand. When I think she's behind that door, right there, and I don't know what she's thinking. And even if you are from the police, all the better. I like dealing with the police. Africa must come as a pretty rude shock to a woman who's never been outside Paris. But the fireworks, they'll knock you out. And I'm going to find out what happened to that damned body too.

Exits.

Scene Two

HORN (*in front of the half-open door*). Leona, are you ready?

LEONA. I'm fixing things up.

HORN *approaches.*

No, no, I'm not fixing things up.

HORN *stops.*

I'm waiting till it stops moving.

HORN. What?

LEONA. Till it stops moving. When it gets dark, it'll be better. It's the same at night, in Paris. I feel a little sick for an hour, the time when it changes from day to night. Besides, babies cry too when the sun goes away. I have some pills to take; I can't let myself forget. (*Sticking her head halfway out the door, she points to the bougainvillaea.*) What are those flowers called?

HORN. I don't know.

LEONA *disappears again.*

Come have a drink.

LEONA. A drink? Oh, no, forbidden. That's all I need, you'd really see me then. It's strictly forbidden for me.

HORN. Come on out anyway.

LEONA. I'm making a list of what's missing. I'm missing a lot of things and I've got loads of things I'll never need. They told me a sweater, Africa is cold at night. Cold, oh yeah, the crooks. So here I am with three sweaters on my hands. I feel so . . . jittery, Cookie, I've got the jitters, butterflies. What are the other men like? People don't like me, generally, the first time.

HORN. There's only one, I already told you.

LEONA. Planes, now there's one thing I don't like. Really, you know, I prefer the phone, you can always hang up. Still, I prepared myself, prepared like crazy. I listened to reggae the whole blessed day, it drove the people in my building nuts. You know what I just discovered, when I opened my suitcase? Parisians have this distinct smell, I knew it. That smell of theirs, I'd smelled it before down in the métro, in the street, off all those people you brush up against, I smelled it hanging and rotting in corners. And I can still smell it, there, in my suitcase. I can't stand it any more. Whenever a sweater, a blouse, any little bit of cloth gets that smell of fish or oil or that hospital smell, try and get it out. And this one's even worse. I'll need time to air out all my things. Oh, I'm so glad I'm here – Africa, at last!

HORN. But you haven't seen anything yet, and you won't even come out of your room.

LEONA. Oh, I've seen enough and I can see enough of it from here to love it. I'm not just visiting. I'm ready now, as soon as I finish my list of what I'm missing and what I have too much of, and air out those clothes, I'll be right out, I promise.

HORN. I'll be waiting for you, Leona.

LEONA. No don't wait for me, no don't wait for me.

The calls of the guard; LEONA appears halfway.

What's that?

HORN. It's the guards. In the evening and at night they call to each other now and then to keep each other awake.

LEONA. It's awful. (*Listens.*) Don't wait for me. (*Goes back in.*) Oh, Cookie? I have a confession to make.

HORN. What?

LEONA (*in a low voice*). Just before leaving, last night, I took a walk along the Seine. And guess what? Suddenly I felt so good, oh, so happy, like never before, for no reason. It's awful. Whenever anything like that happens to me, well, I know something bad's going to happen. I don't like to dream about things that are too happy or feel too good – it puts me in a state for the whole blessed day and I just wait for the worst. I get these intuitions, but they're all upside-down. And they're never wrong. Oh, I'm in no hurry to come out, Cookie.

HORN. You're nervous. It's perfectly normal.

LEONA. You hardly even know me!

HORN. Come on out, come on out now.

LEONA. Are you sure there's only one man?

HORN. Absolutely positive.

LEONA (*her arm appears*). You've left me dying of thirst. When I've had something to drink, I'll come out, I promise.

HORN. I'll get you something to drink.

LEONA. Just some water, really, some water. I have some pills to take, and to take with water.

HORN *leaves; LEONA appears, looks around.*

This is all so overwhelming.

She leans over, picks a flower from the bougainvillaea, and goes back in again.

Scene Three

Below the verandah. HORN enters.

CAL (*at the table, his head in his hands*). Toubab, you poor thing. Why did you leave? (*He cries.*) Did I do something bad to him? Horn, you know me, you know my nerves. If he doesn't come back tonight, I'll kill 'em all. Damn dog eaters! They've taken him from me. I can't sleep without him, Horn.

They're probably eating him right now. I don't even hear any more barking. Toubab!

HORN (*setting out the game of buck dice*). Too much whisky.

He pushes the bottle aside.

CAL. Too much quiet!

HORN. Fifty francs.

CAL (*raising his head*). On five numbers?

HORN. On each one.

CAL. I won't see you that much. Ten francs on each, that's as high as I go.

HORN (*gives him a sudden look*). I see you shaved and combed your hair.

CAL. I always shave at night, you know that.

HORN (*looking at the dice*). It's mine.

He collects.

CAL. Besides, I want to play with chips, for fun, for the pure fun of it. You just rake it in and rake it in, there isn't any pleasure in it any more. The only thing that gives you pleasure is raking in the dough. It's disgusting. Every man for himself and nothing for pleasure. A woman'll add a little humanity to this place. She'll get sick of you soon enough, though. It's the game that interests me, not the money. We should play with chips. Besides, women prefer playing with chips. Women bring humanity to games.

HORN (*in a low voice*). Cal, there's a man over there. He's from the village or the police or worse, because I've never seen him before. He won't say who sent him here, but you can bet he's gonna want an explanation and you're going to give it to him. So get ready. I'm not getting mixed up in it. I have too much on my mind. I don't know anything. I'm not going to cover for you. I wasn't there. My work is done, that's it, goodbye. This time, you'll answer yourself. And you can't even handle a lousy drop of whisky.

CAL. But it's got nothing to do with me, Horn, I didn't do anything, Horn. (*Low.*) This isn't the time to split up, we should stick together, Horn. It's simple, you make out one report for the police, one for the higher-ups, you sign it, and that's that. And me, I keep quiet. Everybody believes *you*, all I've got is my dog, nobody listens to me. It's us against them. I'm not talking to that nigger. It's all very simple, and I'm telling you the truth, it's up to you now. You know my nerves, Horn, you know how bad they are. It's better if I don't see him. And in the first place, I don't want to see anybody till my dog comes back. (*Cries.*) They're gonna eat my dog.

HORN. Fifty francs on each, that's as low as I go.

CAL (*puts down the fifty francs; croaking of toads, close by*). We were looking up at the sky, me and the workers. The dog smelled the storm in the air. This guy started crossing the yard; I see him. Just then, this storm breaks out. I yell, 'Toubab, come here, Toubab!' The dog raises his nose and his fur stands up; he gets the scent of death. The poor thing got all excited. Then I see him running toward the nigger, there, through sheets of rain. 'Toubab, come here,' I yelled; poor dog. Then, in the middle of all the racket, and the flashes of lightning, there was this huge clap of thunder. Toubab froze; everybody was watching. And we see this nigger fall, in this flash of lightning, hit, in tons of rain; and he lays down in the mud. There was this sulphur smell coming toward us; then, the sound of a truck, over there, heading straight at us.

HORN *shakes the dice.*

Toubab's gone, I can't sleep without him, Horn. (*Cries.*) He's slept on me ever since he was little. Instinct's always made him come back, he can't fend for himself, Horn, poor thing. I don't hear him barking. They must have eaten him. At night he'd be a ball of fur on my belly or my legs, or my crotch. It helped me sleep, Horn, he's gotten into my blood. What did I ever do to hurt him?

HORN (*looks at the dice*). Twelve.

CAL *collects.*

CAL (*with a wink*). Some surprise, Horn.

You say, 'I'm going to the airport'; you come back, and you say, 'My wife's here!' Nice move. I didn't even know you finally found one. What's got into you all of a sudden, man?

HORN. A man shouldn't let his life end without putting down roots.

CAL. No, man, of course not. (*Collects.*) What counts is that you make the right choice.

HORN. So the last time I was in Paris I said, 'If you don't find her now, you never will.'

CAL. And you found her! You're a real lady-killer, man! (*They put down their bets.*) But don't forget this climate. It drives women crazy. It's a scientific fact.

HORN. Not this one.

CAL *collects.*

CAL. She's got to have a good pair of shoes, tell her I can lend her a pair. Women dress for style and they don't know anything about African diseases, the ones you get through your feet, man.

HORN. This one's no ordinary woman, no sir.

CAL (*with a wink*). So I'll make a good impression on her. I'll find a chance to kiss her hand or something, show her some real class.

HORN. I said, 'You like fireworks?' 'Yes,' she said, and I said, 'I put one on every year, in Africa, and this one'll be the last. You want to see it?' 'Yes,' she said. So, I gave her the address, the money for the plane fare, 'Be there in a month, that's how long it takes for the package from Ruggieri to get there.' 'Yes,' she said. And that's how I found her. For the last of the fireworks, I wanted a woman who had seen them. (*Puts down his bet.*) I told her the project's closing and that I'll be leaving Africa for good. She said yes to everything. She always says yes.

CAL (*pauses*). Why are they calling off the project, Horn?

HORN. Nobody knows. I put down fifty.

CAL *puts down the money.*

CAL. Why all of a sudden, Horn? Why no explanation? I want to keep on working, Horn. And the work we've done? Half the forest cut down, twenty miles of road? A bridge under construction? And the camp, the wells we dug? All that time for nothing? Why doesn't anybody know anything about what's been decided, Horn? Why don't *you* know?

HORN (*looks at the dice*). It's mine.

Silence. The calls of the guards.

CAL (*in a low voice*). He's grinding his teeth.

HORN. What?

CAL. There, behind the tree, that nigger, tell him to leave, Horn.

Silence; barking in the distance; CAL starts.

Toubab! I hear him. He's hanging around by the sewer. Let him fall in, I'm not gonna budge. (*They bet.*) What kind of shit is this? He just kind of sniffs around and when I call him, he doesn't respond, he pretends like he's thinking it over. Is that him? Yes. Think it over, you mutt, I'm not gonna fish you out. He must have smelled something strange; let him fend for himself; he won't fall in; and even if he does, I'm not moving from here.

They look at the dice. CAL collects. In a low voice.

That other one, Horn, I'm telling you, he wasn't even a real worker; just a day laborer. Nobody knew him, nobody'll ever even mention him. He wants to leave, see, so I say, 'No way, you're not goin' nowhere.' Leave the yard an hour early; an hour's an hour. If you let 'em take an hour, it sets a bad example. Like I'm telling you, I say, 'No.' So he spits at my feet and takes off. He spit at my feet – that much closer and he would have hit my shoe. (*They bet.*) So I call the others and I say, 'Did you see that guy?' (*Imitating an African accent.*) 'Yes, boss, yes, we see.' 'He crossed the yard without waiting for the whistle?' 'Yes, boss, yes, he no wait for whistle,' 'Without his hard hat on, has he got one?' 'No, boss, no, we see him and he no wear his hard hat.' So I say,

'Remember this, he left without my permission.' 'Yes, boss, oh yes, he no have permission.' Then he fell, the truck came through and I asked again, 'Well, who was driving the truck? How fast was he going? Didn't he see that nigger?' And then, bam!

CAL *collects.*

HORN. Everybody saw you shoot him. Idiot, you can't hold your goddamn temper.

CAL. It's like I'm telling you, it wasn't me, he fell.

HORN. He was shot. And everybody saw you get into the truck.

CAL. The shot was the storm; and the truck, that was the rain that blinded everything.

HORN. I may not have been to school, but I could have predicted all this crap you're trying to feed me. You'll see how much good it does you. As for me, count me out, you're an idiot and it's none of my business. A hundred.

CAL. I'll see you.

HORN (*bangs on the table*). Why did you touch it, for God's sake? Whoever touches the body is responsible for the crime, that's how it is in this damned country. If nobody had touched it, nobody would have been responsible, it would have been a crime without a guilty party, what they call a female crime, an accident. The whole business was so simple. But the women came for the body and there was nothing for them to find – nothing, you idiot! (*Bangs the table.*) Get out of this one yourself.

He shakes the dice.

CAL. When I saw him, I said to myself, 'I'm not gonna be able to leave this one alone.' Instinct, Horn, nerves. I didn't even know him. All he did was spit a couple of centimeters from my shoe, but that's how instinct works. 'There's no way I'm gonna be able to leave you in peace now,' that's what I said to myself standing there looking down at him.

So I put him in the truck, I got as far as the dump, and I carried him up and threw him on top: that's exactly what you deserve, I said. And then I came back. But I went back, Horn; I couldn't sit still, my nerves kept working away at me. I hauled him all the way back down off the dump and put him back in the truck: I took him to the lake and I threw him in. But that's what was eating away at me, Horn, just leaving him alone like that in the lake. So I went back, I waded in up to my waist, and I fished him out. He was in the truck and I didn't know what else to do with him, Horn. I won't ever be able to leave you alone, I said, never, it's just stronger than me. I look at him, and I say to myself, 'This boubou's gonna make me a nervous wreck.' And then it came to me: 'The sewer, yeah, that's it! No way you'll go in after him in there.' And that's how it was, Horn, to leave him in peace, despite myself, once and for all. Then I could finally calm down.

They look at the dice.

Horn, if I had buried him, I would have dug him up, I know I would. And if they had taken him to the village, I would have gone after him. The sewer was the simplest solution, Horn, it was the best. Besides, it calmed me down, a little.

HORN *gets up;* CAL *collects.*

And the germs on these niggers, man, nigger germs are the worst. Tell her that, too. Women are never prepared enough for danger.

HORN *exits.*

Scene Four

HORN (*with ALBOURY under the tree*). I just found out he wasn't wearing his hard hat. I was telling you how careless the workers are; I guessed right. No hard hat, that frees us of any responsibility.

ALBOURY. Then give me the body without the hard hat, give it to me the way it is.

HORN. Look, that's what I came to tell you: I'm asking you to choose. Stay or go, but don't stand there in the dark,

behind that tree. It's exasperating to
know there's somebody there. If you
want to come sit with us at the table,
then come, I never said you couldn't.
But if you don't, then go, I'm asking
you. I'll meet with you in the office
tomorrow morning and we'll look into
all this. Actually, I'd prefer you to go.
I never said I didn't want to give you a
glass of whisky, that's not what I said.
So which is it? You refuse to come and
have a drink? You don't want to come
to the office tomorrow morning? So?
You have to choose, mister.

ALBOURY. I wait here to take the
body, that is all I want. And I say that
when I have my brother's body, I will
leave.

HORN. The body, the body! Your body
didn't have a hard hat. There are
witnesses, he crossed the yard without
his hard hat. They won't get a penny,
you tell them that, mister.

ALBOURY. When I take the body back,
I will tell them: no hard hat, not a
penny.

HORN. Think about my wife for a
minute. All this noise, these shadows,
this shouting; everything here is pretty
scary for someone who just got here.
Tomorrow she'll be all settled in, but
tonight . . .! She just got here, so if on
top of that she sees, or thinks she sees
– if there's somebody behind this
tree . . . you have no idea. She'll be
terrified. Is that what you want, you
want to terrorize my wife, mister?

ALBOURY. No, that is not what I want.
I want to take the body back to the
family.

HORN. You tell them this – I'll give the
family a hundred and fifty dollars. And
you, I'll give you two hundred; I'll give
it to you tomorrow. That's a lot. But
this is probably the last death we'll
have around here and then what? So
there you have it. Now go.

ALBOURY. That is what I will tell
them, a hundred and fifty dollars, and
I will take the body with me.

HORN. Tell them, that's right, you tell
them that, that's what they're
interested in. A hundred and fifty
dollars'll shut 'em up. As for the rest,

believe me, it doesn't interest them in
the least. The body, the body, ha!

ALBOURY. It interests me.

HORN. Get out.

ALBOURY. I stay.

HORN. I'll make you go.

ALBOURY. I will not go.

HORN. But you're going to scare my
wife, mister.

ALBOURY. Your wife will not be afraid
of me.

HORN. Oh yes, yes she will; somebody
moving around in the shadows! It'll
end up with me having the guards
shoot you, see, that's what I'll end up
having to do.

ALBOURY. The scorpion you kill
always returns.

HORN. Mister, mister, you're getting
carried away. What are you talking
about? Until now, I've always gotten
along real well . . . Am *I* getting
carried away? You must admit you're
being especially difficult; it's impossible
to deal with you. You have to make an
effort. So stay, stay, since that's what
you seem to want. (*Low.*) I know
they're furious over at the ministry.
But, you understand, I don't have
anything to do with these high-level
decisions. A lowly foreman doesn't
decide anything, I don't have any
authority. Besides, they have to
understand, the government keeps
handing out orders, but it doesn't hand
out any money. It's been months since
they paid anybody anything. The
company can't keep these projects
open if the government doesn't pay.
You understand? I know there's a lot
to be dissatisfied about: bridges
unfinished, roads that go nowhere. But
what can I do, huh? Money, where's
all the money going? The country's
rich, so why is the state's treasury
empty? I'm not saying this to offend
you, but you explain that to me,
mister.

ALBOURY. What they say is that the
government palace has become a den
of iniquity, that they send to France for
expensive champagne and women; that
they drink and fuck there, day and

night, in the offices of the ministers, that's why the treasury is empty, that is what I am told, sir.

HORN. They fuck in the offices! Did you hear that? (*Laughs.*) He's putting down his own government, did you hear that? Hey, you're all right. I don't like these official types and you really don't seem like the official type to me. I really like you. We're going to get along just fine.

ALBOURY. As for me, I wait for someone to give me my brother.

HORN. So tell me. Why does it mean so much to you to get him back? Tell me this man's name again?

ALBOURY. His revealed name was Nouofia; and he had a secret name.

HORN. But his body, what does his body matter to you? This is the first time I hear this. I really thought I understood Africans, how little they value life and death. I'm willing to believe you're especially sensitive, but it really isn't love that makes you so stubborn, is it? Isn't love strictly a European thing?

ALBOURY. No, it is not love.

HORN. I knew it, I knew it. I've noticed this insensitivity over and over. It's shocking to a lot of Europeans. I'm not condemning it, Orientals are even worse. But still, why are you being so stubborn about such a little thing, huh? I told you I'd make it up to you.

ALBOURY. Often little people want a little thing, something very simple, but this little thing is what they want. Nothing will change their minds; and they will let themselves be killed for it. And even when they have been killed, even when they are dead, they want it still.

HORN. Who was he, Alboury, and you – who are you?

ALBOURY. A long time ago, I said to my brother, 'I feel cold.' He said to me, 'It is because there is a little cloud between you and the sun.' I said to him, 'Can it be that this little cloud makes me freeze when all around me men sweat and are scorched by the sun?' My brother said to me, 'I too am cold.' So we warmed ourselves together.

Then I said to my brother, 'When will this cloud go away, that the sun may warm us too?' He answered, 'It will never go away, it will follow us everywhere, forever between us and the sun.' And I felt it following us, everywhere, and among men laughing naked in the heat, my brother and I shivered and warmed ourselves together.

So beneath this little cloud my brother and I grew accustomed to one another. If my back itched, I had my brother there to scratch it, and I scratched his when it itched him; in my distress I bit the nails of his hand and in his sleep, he sucked the thumb of my hand.

The women we had clung to us and they too began to grow cold, and the shivering that seized one of us rippled like a wave through all the rest. Mothers came to join us and the mothers of mothers and their children and our children, a family of untold numbers from whom not even the dead are torn away, but kept close among us.

The little cloud rose higher and higher toward the sun, depriving of all warmth a family that grew larger and larger, that grew more and more accustomed to one another, a numberless family of corpses, living and to come, each indispensable to the other, as we watched the land about us still warmed by the sun shrink and grow small.

That is why I have come to claim my brother's body, which has been torn from us, because his absence has destroyed this closeness which keeps us warm, because even dead, we need his warmth to warm ourselves, and he needs ours as we need his.

HORN. It's hard for us to understand each other.

They stare at each other.

I think it'll always be hard to live together whatever we do.

Silence.

ALBOURY. I was told that in America blacks go out in the morning and whites go out in the afternoon.

HORN. Is that what you were told?

ALBOURY. If it is true, sir, it is a very good idea.

HORN. You really think so?

ALBOURY. Yes.

HORN. No, it's a very bad idea. We have to co-operate. On the contrary, Mr Alboury, we have to force people to co-operate. That's my idea.

All right, my good Mr Alboury, listen to this. I have a terrific plan of my own that I've never told anybody about. You're the first. Tell me what you think of it. You know these three billion human beings they're always making such a stink about? The way I figure, if you house them all in forty-storey buildings – I have yet to decide on the style of the architecture, but forty storeys, and not one more, is plenty tall – in average-sized apartments, my figures make sense. These buildings would make up a city whose streets would be ten metres wide, which is just right. Now this city would cover half of France, not one square kilometre more. All the rest would be empty, completely empty. You can check my figures, I've been over them a dozen times, they're absolutely correct. You think my plan sounds stupid? The only thing left is choosing the site for this unique city, and the problem would be solved. No more fights, no more rich countries, no more poor countries, everybody under the same flag, and the world's resources for everybody. You see, Alboury, I'm something of a communist too, in my own way.

France seems ideal to me. It's a temperate country, good rainfall, no extremes in weather, vegetation, animals, health hazards; ideal, France is ideal. It certainly could be built in the southern part, the sunniest part. Me, I like the winter, good old rough winters; you don't know what a good old rough winter is, mister. It'd be best to build it, this city, lengthwise, from Germany to Spain, running along the Alps; people who like winter would live around what used to be Strasbourg and people who can't stand snow,

asthmatics and people sensitive to the cold, would live where Marseille and Bayonne had been torn down. The last of humanity's conflicts would be a theoretical debate over the advantages of winter in Alsace as opposed to those of spring on the Riviera. As for the rest of the world, well sir, it would be a kind of preserve. Think of it! A free Africa! Her wealth would be exploited, underground, above ground, solar energy, without bothering a soul. And Africa alone would be enough to feed my city for generations, before anybody would have to set foot in Asia or America. Technology would be used to maximum benefit, workers would be kept to a strict minimum, in well-organized shifts, something like a civil service. And they would bring back the oil, gold, uranium, coffee, bananas, everything you want, without a single African suffering foreign invasion, because they won't be there any more! Yes, France would be beautiful, open to the peoples of the world, everyone mingling together as they strolled through the streets; and Africa would be beautiful, empty abundant, free from suffering, the breast of the world!

My plan makes you laugh? At least it's an idea, and a more brotherly one than yours. That's how I want to think and how I'll go on thinking.

They stare at each other. The wind rises.

Scene Five

Below the verandah.

CAL (*spots* LEONA, *shouts*). Horn!

He takes a drink.

LEONA. What do you call these flowers?

CAL. Horn!

LEONA. Do you know where I could find something to drink?

CAL. Horn!

Drinks.

What the hell is he doing?

LEONA. Don't call him, don't bother. I'll find it by myself.

She walks off.

CAL (*stops her*). You plan to walk around here in those shoes?

LEONA. My shoes?

CAL. Sit down. So what's the matter, do I scare you?

LEONA. No.

Silence; a dog barks in the distance.

CAL. They don't know what shoes are in Paris. They don't know anything in Paris. They just make fashion, no matter how.

LEONA. They're the only thing I bought myself, and here you're telling me this. Those crooks, and the price they make you pay, for a little scrap of leather. Saint Laurent, 'Boutique Afrique', no less. And expensive! Oh. Such extravagance!

CAL. They should come up higher, they have to give your ankles some support. If you have a good pair of shoes, you'll make it, they're the most important thing, shoes are.

He takes a drink.

LEONA. Yes.

CAL. If it's sweat you're afraid of, well, forget it; one layer dries, and then after that another one, and another, it forms a kind of shell, a protective shell. And if it's the smell you're afraid of, smells help develop your instincts. Besides, when you know the smell, you know the man, and it's very practical too, you can tell what belongs to who, everything becomes much simpler, it's an instinct, that's all.

LEONA. Oh yes.

Silence.

CAL. Have a drink. Why aren't you drinking?

LEONA. Whisky? Oh, no, I can't. My pills. And then, I'm not that thirsty.

CAL. Around here you have to drink, thirsty or not; if you don't you dry up.

He drinks. Silence.

LEONA. I have a button I should sew on. It's just like me; button-holes, no, they're just too much for me. No patience, none. I always leave them till the end and, and finally, well, there it is, a safety-pin. The fanciest dresses I've made myself, I swear, it's still and always will be a safety-pin they're fastened with. One of these days, Missy, you'll prick yourself.

CAL. I was the same way before, with whisky, I turned my nose up at it; and I drank milk, me, nothing but milk, I'm telling you; litres, barrels; before I started travelling. But since then, hell, all their crappy powdered milk, all their American milk, their soy milk, no cow ever had anything to do with any of it. So there's no choice but to turn to this crap.

He drinks.

LEONA. Yes.

CAL. Luckily, this crap here can be found everywhere, this stuff can. I've never had to do without it, anywhere in the world. And I've done some travelling, believe you me. Have you travelled much?

LEONA. Oh, no, this is the very first time.

CAL. Young as I look, I've travelled, believe me, believe me. I've been to Bangkok; I've been to Isfahan; the Black Sea; Marrakesh and Tangiers; Reunion; I've been to the Caribbean; Honolulu; Vancouver; Brazil; Colombia; Patagonia; the Baleares; Guatemala; Chicoutimi, me; and finally, this crap-heap here, Africa. Dakar, Abidjan, Lome, Leopoldville, Johannesburg, Lagos. Africa's the worst of all, I can tell you that. And everywhere you go, whisky and soy milk; and no surprises. Still, I'm young; and let me tell you this, one whisky's like every other, one job like the next, one French company like every other French company, all the same old crap.

LEONA. Oh yes oh no.

CAL. Drink this.

He holds out a glass of whisky.

LEONA. So where is he then?

Silence.

CAL (*in a low voice*). Why did you come here?

LEONA (*startled*). Why? I wanted to see Africa.

CAL. To see what? (*Pause.*) This here isn't Africa. It's a French public works project, babe.

LEONA. But it's still . . .

CAL. No. Horn interests you?

LEONA. We're supposed to get married, yes.

CAL. To Horn? get married to Horn?

LEONA. Yes, yes, to him.

CAL. No.

LEONA. Why do you always say . . . Where is Cookie?

CAL. Cookie? (*Laughs.*) Horn can't get married. You know that, don't you. (*Silence.*) He must have told you about . . .

LEONA. Yes, yes, he told me about . . . that.

CAL. So he told you about that, huh?

LEONA. Yes, yes.

CAL. That Horn's a brave man. (*Drinks.*) To stay here all alone for a month, all alone with a few boubous; to guard the supplies, during their shitty little war; you couldn't have gotten me to do it. So, he told you everything, the run-in with the looters, his, uh, wound – terrible wound – and everything? (*Drinks.*) Horn's a real gambler.

LEONA. Yes.

CAL. No. What's it getting him now? What more has he got out of it? You know?

LEONA. No, I don't know.

CAL (*with a wink*). But you must know what he's got less of! (*Drinks.*) There's something funny about that story. (*Looks at her.*) What is it about you that interests him?

The call of the guards. Silence.

LEONA. I'm too thirsty.

She gets up, walks off under the trees.

Scene Six

The wind stirs up a red dust; LEONA sees someone beneath the bougainvillaea. In the murmuring and sighing of the wind, in the flapping of wings that surrounds her, she seems to hear her name, then she feels the pain of a tribal mark graven on to her cheek.

The Harmattan, the wind of sands, carries her to the foot of the tree.

LEONA (*walking up to ALBOURY*). I'm looking for some water. *Wasser, bitte.* (*Laughs.*) Do you understand German? It's the only other language I know a little of. You see, my mother was German, really German, one hundred per cent, and my father Alsatian, so with all that, I . . . (*Moves toward the tree.*) They must be looking for me. (*Looks at ALBOURY.*) But he told me that . . . (*Softly.*) *Dich erkenne ich, es ist sicher.* (*Looks around her.*) It was when I saw the flowers that I recognized everything; I recognized these flowers whose name I don't know. But they used to hang like this from the branches in my head, and all the colours, I already had them in my head. Do you believe in reincarnation? (*Looks at him.*) Why did he tell me there was nobody else but them? (*Upset.*) I believe in it, I do, I believe in it. Moments so happy, so very happy, that come back to me from so far away; so sweet. It must all be very old. I do believe in it. I've spent one life on the edge of a lake somewhere, already, and it keeps coming back to me, in my head. (*Shows him a bougainvillaea blossom.*) These flowers, you only find them in hot countries, is that right? But now I recognized them, coming from far away, and I'm looking for the rest, the warm water of the lake, the happy moments. (*Very upset.*) I've already been buried under a little yellow rock, somewhere, beneath flowers like these. (*Leans toward him.*) He told me there was no one else. (*Laughs.*) And there's you! (*Moves away.*) It's going to rain, isn't it? So tell me, what are the insects going to do when it rains?

One drop of water on their wings and that's it for them. So what's going to happen to them, in the rain? (*Laughs.*)

I'm really glad you're not French or anything like that. This way you won't take me for a fool. Besides, I'm not really French either. Half German, half Alsatian. Hey, we were made for . . . I'll learn your African language, yes, and when I speak it right, carefully choosing every word I say, I'll say . . . things, important things . . . to you . . . things that . . . I don't know. I don't dare look at you any more; you're so serious, and me, serious! (*Moves about excitedly.*) Can you feel the wind? When the wind shifts like this, it's the devil turning around. *Verschwinde, Teufel, pchtt*, go away. Then, they rang the cathedral bells, to make the devil go away, when I was little. There's no cathedral here? It's funny, a country without a cathedral. I like cathedrals. But there's you, so serious. I really like seriousness. (*Laughs.*) I'm such a dummy. Sorry. (*Stops moving around.*) I'd rather stay here; it's so sweet. (*Touches him without looking at him.*) *Komm mit mir, Wasser holen.* What a dummy. I'm sure they're out looking for me; but there's nothing for me to do with them, that's for sure. (*Lets go of him.*) Someone's there. I heard . . . (*Low.*) *Teufel! Verschwinde, pchttt!* (*In his ear.*) I'll be back. Wait for me.

ALBOURY *disappears into the trees.*

Oder Sie, kommen Sie zurück!

Enter CAL.

Scene Seven

CAL (*a finger up to his lips*). Don't talk too loud, babe. He wouldn't like it.

LEONA. Who? There's nobody here but us.

CAL. That's right, baby, that's right, nobody but us. (*Laughs.*) Horn's a jealous man.

Barking close by.

Toubab! What's he doing up so close? (*Grabs* LEONA *by the arm.*) Was there somebody else over here?

LEONA. Who's Toubab?

CAL. My dog. He barks whenever he sees a boubou. Did you see somebody?

LEONA. Did you train him?

CAL. Train him? I never trained my dog. It's instinct; he doesn't need any training. You just be careful if you see anything. Let the animals settle things between themselves. You run and get inside.

LEONA. What? If I see what?

CAL. What you'll get by asking questions instead of running is a bullet in your gut or a knife in your back. I'm telling you, no matter what you see, if you haven't seen it before or I haven't shown it to you, you run real fast and get inside where it's safe. (*Takes* LEONA *in his arms.*) Poor little thing. One day I got here just like you, full of ideas about Africa, what I'd see, what I'd hear. I loved it in my head. You don't see anything, you don't hear anything you thought you would. I understand why you're sad.

LEONA. I'm not sad. I was looking for something to drink, that's all.

CAL. What did you say your name was?

LEONA. Leona.

CAL. Is it the money you're interested in?

LEONA. What money? What are you talking about?

CAL *lets go of her, walks over to the truck.*

CAL. This woman's a fox, she's dangerous. (*Laughs.*) What kind of work did you do, in Paris?

LEONA. In a hotel. Chambermaid.

CAL. Servant girl. You make less than you think here.

LEONA. I don't think anything.

CAL. You work hard and you don't make anything.

LEONA. Yes you do, I know you make a lot.

CAL. And just where did the little servant girl hear that? Do I seem to you like I make a lot of money? (*Shows her his hands.*) Do I seem to you like somebody who doesn't work?

LEONA. It's not because you work that you're rich.

CAL. Rich is not having to wreck your hands like this, that's rich. Being rich solves everything, no more troubles, no more sweat, you don't have to lift a finger, you don't have to do anything you don't want to do. No pain. That's rich. But us? Get it out of your head. Yeah, they pay, but not enough, not nearly enough. Really rich people don't suffer at all. (*Looks at* LEONA.) His little adventure during the war here, and that . . . accident must have earned Horn a lot of money. He never talks about it so it must be a hell of a lot. So money interests you, huh, baby?

LEONA. Don't call me baby. You have these words: boubou, baby, your dog's name. Why do you have to call everybody by dogs' names? Money isn't what made me follow Cookie here, no.

CAL. So, why did you?

LEONA. I followed him here because he suggested it to me.

CAL. So if just anybody had suggested it to you, you would have followed him, is that it? (*Laughs*.) This is one hot woman!

LEONA. It wasn't just anybody.

CAL. And you like fireworks, too, don't you, baby?

LEONA. Yes, that too, he told me about that too.

CAL. You're a dreamer, aren't you? And you'd like to make me dream too, wouldn't you? (*Rough*.) Well, I dream the truth, I don't dream lies. (*Looks at her*.) This woman's a thief.

LEONA *gives a start;* CAL *draws her into his arms again.*

I'm just having a little fun, babe, don't get upset. We haven't seen a woman around here for so long, I'd just like to have a little fun. I seem like a savage to you, don't I?

LEONA. No, oh . . .

CAL. Sure, we could turn into savages if we let ourselves go. But just because you find yourself in the bottom of a hole like this isn't any reason to let yourself give in to it, that's what I say.

Take me, for instance, I'm interested in lots of things, you'll see. I like to talk, have a good time, and I like to exchange ideas most of all. Hey, I was crazy about philosophy, actually. But how much of that is there around here? No, Africa isn't what you think it is. And the old guys here don't want us bringing in any new ideas. What with the company, the work, it doesn't leave much time. Ideas, though, I've still got a few ideas; I had some. But always thinking, thinking, all by yourself, you end up feeling the ideas explode in your head, one by one. As soon as I get one going, pop, like a balloon. Pop! You probably saw them, on the way in, along the side of the road, the dogs, their bellies swollen up like balloons, and their paws in the air. But what counts is being able to exchange ideas with somebody. I've always been the curious type, music, philosophy, Troyat, Zola, especially Miller, Henry. You can come to my room and pick out some books, I've got all of Miller, my books are your books. What did you say your name was?

LEONA. Leona.

CAL. I was really wild about philosophy, when I was a student. Especially Miller, Henry. Reading him totally blew me away. I went wild in Paris. Paris, the crossroads of the world's ideas. Yeah, Miller. When he has the dream where he kills Sheldon with a shot from a pistol and says, 'I'm not a Polack!' Do you know it?

LEONA. I don't know . . . No.

CAL. So when you come here, there's no way you can just let yourself go, no way, baby.

LEONA. Leona.

CAL. This woman is really defensive with me. (*Laughs*.) There's no need, you just have to say what's on your mind. Nothing stands between us, we're the same age, we're a lot alike; anyway, I always say exactly what's on my mind. There's no reason to be uptight.

LEONA. No, there's no reason.

CAL. And then again, we don't have any choice, we're all alone; you won't find nobody to talk to around here, nobody; this here is one godforsaken place. Especially now that it's the end. There's nobody left but me and him. And as for him, he's not particularly . . . well-read, and besides, he's an old man.

LEONA. Old! I like talking to him.

CAL. Yeah, maybe. No. But, in the long run, you need somebody to look up to, to admire. It's very important to admire somebody. Women admire a man for his brains. What's your name?

LEONA. Leona, Leona.

CAL. So?

LEONA. So what?

CAL. Why Horn?

LEONA. Why what?

CAL. You mean you could marry a man who's missing . . . the main thing? You'd do that, for the money? This woman's disgusting!

LEONA. Let me go.

CAL. Come on, baby, I only wanted to see how you'd react. After all, it's your business, not mine. Are you crying or what? Don't take it like that. I understand, you're sad. But am I sad? Believe me, I have every reason in the world to be sad, good reasons too. (*Softly.*) I'll lend you my shoes. All you need is to catch some filthy disease. You almost turn into savages here, I know, because this is the world turned upside-down. But that's no reason to cry. Look at me, I have more degrees and more qualifications than Horn, but he's still in charge. Does that sound right to you? Everything's upside down here. But do I belly-ache about it? Do you see me crying?

LEONA. Here's Cookie.

She gets up.

CAL. Don't move. A thief's gotten into the camp. It's dangerous.

LEONA. You see thieves everywhere.

CAL. A boubou thief. The guards let him in by mistake. You barely have time to see them and you're done for, bam! In the belly or the back, bam! Get in the truck.

LEONA. No.

She pushes him away.

CAL. I was just trying to protect you. (*Pause.*) You think I'm bad, I know, baby. But we haven't seen a woman around here since the project started. So seeing one, seeing you, has got me a little nervous, that's all. It's hard for you to understand, you're from Paris. But seeing you, I'm all turned around. I really wish I wasn't like this, I had this feeling we'd like each other right away. But the way I am is never the way I'd like to be. But I'm sure we'll get along just fine. I have good instincts when it comes to women.

He takes her hand.

LEONA. I feel all flushed, oh!

CAL. You're hot-blooded, I saw it right away. I like that, I like a woman who's hot-blooded. We're a lot alike, you know that? (*Laughs.*) This woman is very attractive.

LEONA. The women here must be so beautiful. Oh, I feel so ugly. (*Gets up.*) Here's Cookie now.

CAL (*joins her*). Don't be so modest, little maid. I have good instincts, for certain things.

LEONA (*looks at him*). I think we're so ugly! There he is. I hear him. He's looking for me.

CAL holds her tightly; she finally struggles free.

CAL. Prude!

LEONA. Bully!

CAL. Paris, the biggest whorehouse in the world!

LEONA (*from a distance*). Verschwinde, verschwinde!

CAL. Shit! (*Pause.*) When you haven't seen a woman for so long, you expect . . . as if there was going to be . . . an explosion. And then nothing, not a goddamn thing. Just one more night wasted.

He walks off.

Scene Eight

At the table; on it, the game of buck dice.

HORN. Balance, that's the word. Like with food, the right amount of protein and vitamins, the right amount of fats and calories, a balanced diet, putting together the appetisers, the main course, the desserts. That's how a good fireworks display should be put together, in balance; putting together the colours, a sense of harmony, the right size, the right height for each successive explosion. Balancing the whole thing and balancing each moment, it's a real brain teaser, let me tell you, But you'll see, Cal, what Ruggieri and I, what we do to the sky, you'll see!

CAL. I think this game is idiotic.

HORN. Idiotic? And what's so idiotic about it?

CAL. I think it's idiotic.

HORN. I don't see why you think that, for God's sake.

CAL. That's just it, there's nothing to see, nothing.

HORN. And what would you rather do, for Christ sake? There's just the two of us, what else is there for two people to play? Maybe it's not complicated enough, for you. We can make it more complicated, you know, I know some variations. You set up a bank, and you can only bet on . . .

CAL. The more complicated this game is, the more idiotic it gets.

HORN. So you're not playing any more?

CAL. I don't want to play any more. I feel like an idiot playing this game.

HORN (*after a pause*). No, I'm sorry, but I don't understand.

CAL (*his head in his hands*). Bam!

HORN. What?

CAL. Every time we play this game, after a while, it's like neither of us is playing with a full deck.

He hits his head with his hands.

And it gets me right here, you know?

HORN. What's eating you? They play

everywhere, in all the camps, and I've never seen anybody, anywhere, stop in the middle and say, 'It's like neither of us is playing with a full deck.' What does that mean, for Christ sake? And you either, I've watched you play this game for months . . . If you want, I'll go look for her and we can get up a little game of . . .

CAL. No, no. No poker, no way!

HORN. Because cards don't . . .

CAL. Cards are even more idiotic, no.

HORN. So everybody who plays cards is an idiot? People have been playing cards, for centuries, all over the world; they're idiots and nobody's realised it till now but you. Christ!

CAL. No, no, no. I don't want to play anything any more.

HORN. Well then, what do you suggest we do?

CAL. I don't know. Try not to be idiotic.

HORN. Well, great, let's do it.

They sulk.

CAL (*after a pause*). And this is the sound of Africa. Is it drums? Is it the grinding of grain? No. Here, above the table, it's a fan. And the sound of cards, or a dice shaker. (*Pause. Then in a low voice.*) Amsterdam, London, Vienna, Cracow . . .

HORN. What?

CAL. There are all those cities, north of here I'd like to see . . .

Pause. They pour themselves drinks.

Five francs on the ten.

HORN. With or without a bank?

CAL. No, no, no, simple as possible.

HORN. I'll see you.

They roll the dice. HORN *pushes the bottle of whisky aside.*

It's because you drink too much.

CAL. Too much? No way. I never get loaded, never.

HORN. What the hell is she doing, anyway? Where is she, for Christ sake?

CAL. How should I know? (*Collects.*)

Just the opposite, drunks have always disgusted me. In fact, that's exactly why I like it here. It's always made me sick to be around a drunk. That's why I'd like, yeah, I'd like for the next project . . . (*They place their bets.*) In some of these places I'd be tripping over some stinking drunk every night. I know that kind of stuff goes on. I would be, I know I would. (*They roll the dice.*) You could ask to have me with you on the next project. You've got enough clout, man; you've been at it long enough. They'll listen to you, man.

HORN. There isn't going to be a next project, not for me.

CAL. Of course there is, you know there is, you know damn well there is. Can you really see yourself in some little house, in France, in the south, with some whining woman and a little garden? You'll never leave Africa. (*Collects.*) It's in your blood. (*Pause.*) Don't think I want to flatter you or anything, but first of all, being boss is in your blood. You've got to admit, you're the kind of boss guys get attached to. They get used to you. That's what makes a good boss. I'm used to you, you're my boss, naturally, I don't think twice about it, there's nothing more to say. Out in the yard, when somebody says to me, 'Boss this, boss that,' I always say, 'Hey look, Horn's the boss, not me.' What am I? Nothing. I'm nothing. I'm not ashamed to say it. Without you, nothing at all. You, you're not afraid of anything. You're not even afraid of the cops. But me, without you, well . . . I get scared, I'm not ashamed to admit it. And I mean scared. I see a boubou cop and I turn tail. That's just how it is. I see a regular boubou, I want to shoot. It's all a question of nerves, there's nothing you can do about fear. Even around a woman, I'd panic man, it wouldn't surprise me. That's why I need you. (*Low.*) Everything's falling apart around here. It isn't like it used to be. People come and go, so if we split up, we'll be alone, on top of everything else. (*Lower.*) Don't you think it was a crazy thing to do to bring a woman here? And that nigger, don't you think he came here because there's a woman

around? (*They place their bets.*) We should stick together, Horn. Just the idea of finding myself on another project, surrounded by drunks every night, I'm telling you, I'd shoot up the place, I know I would.

They look at the dice. CAL *collects his winnings.*

HORN (*gets up*). What the hell is she doing, for Christ sake?

CAL. One more round, boss. This one'll be the last. (*Smiles.*) A thousand francs on the ten.

He puts down the money. HORN *hesitates.*

Come on, man, an old gambler like you? You don't have to think about it, do you?

HORN *puts down the money; they roll the dice.*

Wait.

They listen.

He's talking.

HORN. What?

CAL. Behind the tree. He's still there and he's talking.

They listen. A sudden gust of wind, the leaves flutter and then are still again. The dull sound of running, naked feet on stone, in the distance. Leaves and spider webs fall. Silence.

Scene Nine

ALBOURY *crouched down under the bougainvillaea.* LEONA *enters; she crouches down, facing* ALBOURY, *at a certain distance.*

ALBOURY. *Mann na la wax dara?*

LEONA. 'Wer reitet so spät durch Nacht und Wind . . .'

ALBOURY. *Wala niou noppi tè xolan tè rèk.*

LEONA. 'Es ist der Vater mit seinem Kind.' (*Laughs.*) You see, I speak a foreign language too. We'll understand each other in the end, I'm sure.

ALBOURY. *Yaw dégoulo sama lakka wandé man déguana sa boss.*

LEONA. Yes, yes, that's it, that's how we have to speak, you'll see, I'll get it eventually. But you understand me, don't you? If I speak very softly? There's no reason to be afraid of foreign languages, just the opposite. I've always thought that if you watch people carefully for a long time while they're speaking, you understand everything. It takes time and then you have it. I'll speak to you in a foreign language and you do the same, then we'll both be on the same wavelength in no time.

ALBOURY. *Wax guamma déloussil mangui ni.*

LEONA. But slowly, OK? Otherwise, we'll never get anywhere.

ALBOURY (*after a pause*). *Dégoulo ay youxou jiguène?*

LEONA. 'Siehst, Vater, du den Erlkönig nicht?'

ALBOURY. *Man dé déguena ay jioyou jiguène.*

LEONA. ' . . . Der Erlen König mit Kron und Schweif?'

ALBOURY. *You n'guèlaw lidi andi fi.*

LEONA. ' . . . Mein Sohn, es ist ein Nebelstreif.' It's coming, isn't it? you see. Oh, of course, the grammar takes more time, you have to spend a lot of time together for it to be perfect; but even with mistakes . . . What counts is a minimum of vocabulary; not even. It's the tone that counts. No, it's not that, either. Just looking at each other, for a little while, without talking, is enough.

Pause. They look at each other; a dog barks far off in the distance. She laughs.

No, I can't stop talking, we'll stop talking when we understand each other. But there you are, I don't know what to say. And I'm a terrible chatterbox, usually. But when I look at you . . . You impress me; I like being impressed. You now, it's your turn to say something, please.

ALBOURY. *Yaw lay guiss, wandè si sama bir xalatt, bènèn jiguène boudi jouye de terrè wa dèkk bi nèlaw layguiss.*

LEONA. More, more, but slower.

ALBOURY. *Dioye yan n'quimaye tanxale.*

LEONA (*Low*). You're the only one here who looks at me when you talk.

ALBOURY. *Degoulo dioyou jiguène diodiou?*

LEONA. Yes, yes, you see. I really wonder why I came here. I'm afraid of them all, now. (*Smiles at him.*) Except you. And just my luck, that in your own language, I still don't understand a thing, nothing, nothing, nothing.

In deep silence, two guards call out to one another suddenly, brutally; then all is quiet again.

Too bad, I'd like to stay with you anyway. I feel like such a stranger.

ALBOURY. *Lann nga niaw utt si fi?*

LEONA. I think I'm beginning to understand you.

ALBOURY. *Lann nga naw deff si fi?*

LEONA. Yes, oh, I knew it would happen!

ALBOURY. Are you afraid?

LEONA. No.

Suddenly a whirlwind of red dust carrying the howling of dogs flattens the grass and bends the branches, and rising from the ground like an inverted rain, a cloud of mayflies, crazed and suicidal, blots out all light.

Scene Ten

At the table.

CAL. Just another wasted night, another night spent waiting. You don't think it's been a strange night? We quit playing and then we start up again, we wait for this woman and she disappears, and even a fireworks show. But right now, this is the big show Africa puts on, – a cloud of dead bugs.

HORN (*Examines one of the insects*). It is strange, you know. It hasn't rained. They usually come out after it rains. I'll never understand this damn country.

CAL. What a waste, this is what you call a real waste. This woman ignores you completely. She's probably off in some corner crying or who knows what. It doesn't surprise me. I sensed it as soon as I saw her, instinct, you know. I don't want to upset you, man, far from it. I mean your money's your own, you do whatever you want with it, it's yours, nobody else's, you can pay for whatever pleasures you want, man. Only, you don't count on women for pleasure in this life; women, forget it. We have to count on ourselves, ourselves and nobody else, and tell them once and for all that guys like us get more pleasure, a lot more pleasure, from good hard work well done. And you're not going to tell me different, either, man. That's real pleasure no woman'll ever be worth – a good solid bridge built with our own hands and heads, a nice straight road that can hold up to the rainy season, yeah, that's pleasure. Women will never understand anything about what gives a man pleasure. You going to tell me different, man? I know damn well you're not.

HORN. I don't know, maybe, maybe you're right. I remember the first bridge I ever built. The first night, after the last girder was in place, and all the finishing touches had been put on, the night before the official opening. I remember stripping and having this urge to lay down, naked, on the bridge, all night long. I could have broken my neck ten different times that night. I touched every part of that damn bridge, I shinnied up the cables, and there were times, I saw the whole thing, in the moonlight, above the mud, white, I can still remember how white it was.

CAL. Yeah, but you're walking out on this one. What a waste!

HORN. There's nothing I can do about it.

CAL. I should have followed my first impulse and gone into oil, yeah, that was my dream. Oil's got class, you know, a little nobility. Look at the people who work in oil, the way they look down on us. They know damn well they're the top of the heap. Yeah,

oil's always fascinated me, everything that comes from underground's always fascinated me. Bridges make me sick, now. Us guys in public works, what are we? Nothing, next to oil workers, miserable, next to nothing. All our work out in the open, like stupid fools, for the whole world to see, and a hiring policy that says only the unqualified need apply. What kind of man works here? Men who haul and carry and drag things around. Jackasses, elephants, beasts of burden, all of us, we're the dumping ground for any guy who comes along with absolutely no qualifications. But in oil, ah, six or seven qualified men and watch, watch the fortune that runs through their fingers. That's what I've become too, a beast of burden. But I've got qualifications, damn it, I'm qualified! But I need to put all my skills to use. In the evening, when I see those flares down there, in the oil fields, I could look at them for hours.

HORN (bets). Play.

CAL. My heart's not in it, man, my heart's just not in it. (Low.) So you're really walking out on me, is that the idea, Horn? Tell me, tell me. You're walking out on me, aren't you?

HORN. What?

CAL. Tell the guards to shoot him. We've got our rights, goddammit.

HORN. Don't get yourself all worked up over it. Just play and don't worry about it.

CAL. Why did you talk to him? What did you two say? Why don't you have him thrown out. Shit!

HORN. This one's not like the others.

CAL. I knew it. You've been had. I'd really like to know what you two said to each other. Anyway, you're walking out on me, I understand.

HORN. Idiot. You don't understand that in the end I'm going to fuck him over and that'll be the end of it.

CAL. You're going to fuck him over?

HORN. I'm going to fuck him over.

CAL. Just the same, I think you're acting pretty strange with this nigger.

HORN. Jesus Christ, who's in charge around here, anyway?

CAL. You, man, nobody's saying you're not. But still . . .

HORN. Who's in charge of cleaning up everybody else's messes? Who's in charge of running everything, all the time, everywhere, from one end of this camp to the other, from morning to night? Who always has to keep everything in his head, from the smallest part for the smallest truck to how many bottles of whisky are left? Who has to plan everything, make all the decisions, oversee everything, day and night? Who has to play cop, mayor, manager, general, head of the house?

CAL. You, of course, man, you.

HORN. And who has had it, I mean definitely had it?

CAL. You, man.

HORN. It's true, I may not have any fancy degrees, but I'm still the boss, I'm still boss around here.

CAL. Man, I'm not trying to make you mad. All I wanted to say, out of the blue, just like that, was that I thought you were acting strange with this nigger, Horn, to talk to him like normal and . . . strange, that's all. But if you say you're going to fuck him over, well then, you're going to fuck him over.

HORN. The whole thing's practically taken care of already.

CAL (after a pause). Just the same, you're a strange guy. Let me take care of him, it'd be a lot faster.

HORN. You're not taking care of anything. I am.

CAL. You sure have a strange way of going about things.

HORN. There are other ways of defending yourself besides guns, for God sake. I know how to talk to people, how to use words. Maybe I haven't been to school, but I know how to use politics. The only thing you know how to use is a pop-gun and afterwards you're glad if somebody's there to get you out of the mess and watch you cry. So what they teach you in those engineering schools is how to shoot people, not how to talk with them? Terrific! Well, you just do whatever you want, you just go around shooting off your gun whenever you feel like it, and then come crying to me. I'm telling you, this is the last time; after this, I'm leaving. And after I'm gone, you can do whatever the hell you want.

CAL. Hey, man, you don't have to get mad at me.

HORN. All you engineers ever learned in your fancy schools was how to wreck things. Well you just go right on with all your wrecking. Go on, Mr Engineer, and you'll have all Africa hating you. And in the end you won't get a thing for it, nothing, nothing, nothing. You've got a big mouth and an itchy trigger finger and an appetite for easy money. Well, Mr Engineer, I'm telling you, you'll end up with nothing. Did you hear me? Nothing. You people don't give a damn about Africa, all you think about is taking as much as you can, you don't give anything, never, you can't ever give anything. Yeah, well, in the end you'll be left with nothing, nothing at all. And our Africa, you, you and your fancy, educated sons of bitches will have completely wrecked it.

CAL. I don't want to wreck anything, Horn.

HORN. You don't want to love Africa.

CAL. I do love it, I do. Otherwise, I wouldn't be here.

HORN. Just play.

CAL. I don't feel like playing now. With the threat, right here, in the middle of the camp, of some boubou giving it to you in the back, uh-huh, it's got my nerves all rattled. What I think is he came here to cash in on this whole thing and stir up trouble. That's how I see it.

HORN. You don't see anything. He wants to make an impression. It's politics.

CAL. Or else it's for the woman, like I said at first.

HORN. No, he's got something else on his mind.

CAL. His mind? What mind? What else does a boubou have on his mind? You're walking out on me, I saw it right away.

HORN. I can't walk out on you, you idiot.

CAL. You could prove it was an accident, Horn, will you prove it?

HORN. Yeah, an accident. Why not? Who said it wasn't?

CAL. I knew it. It's best if we stick together. We can get 'em if we stick together. I understand now. You talk things over so you can fuck him over. That's one way of doing things, I must admit. But look out just the same, Horn. Your way you risk finding yourself with a piece of lead in your belly.

HORN. He's unarmed.

CAL. Yeah, well all the same, you better watch out. These bastards all know karate and they're all strong, all these bastards. You could be laid flat before you even open your mouth.

HORN (*shows him two bottles of whisky*). I'm armed. Nobody can resist whisky like this.

CAL. Don't you think a couple of beers would be enough?

HORN. Play.

CAL (*places bet, sighing*). What a waste.

HORN. While I'm talking to him, you go get the body. Don't ask any questions, do whatever you have to, just get the body. Look for it, I've got to have it. If not, the whole village'll be on our backs. Find it by morning or else you're on your own, for good.

CAL. No, it's impossible, no. I'll never find it. I can't.

HORN. Just find one, any one.

CAL. But how? how am I supposed to do that?

HORN. It shouldn't be too far.

CAL. No, Horn!

HORN (*looks at the dice*). It's mine.

CAL. The way you're handling this stinks!

He comes down with his fist in the middle of the game.

You're an asshole, a real asshole.

HORN (*Gets up*). Do what I say. Or else I'll drop the whole thing.

Exit.

CAL. That bastard's walking out on me. I'm finished.

Scene Eleven

At the construction site, at the foot of the uncompleted bridge near the river, in half darkness, ALBOURY *and* LEONA.

LEONA. Your hair is super.

ALBOURY. They say our hair is black and charred because one day the first father of blacks, abandoned by God and then by all other men, found himself alone with the devil. The devil too had been abandoned by all. As a sign of friendship, he caressed the first father's head, and that is how our hair was burnt.

LEONA. Oh, I love stories with the devil. I love the way you tell them. Your lips are just super. Besides, black's my colour.

ALBOURY. It is a good colour to hide in.

LEONA. What's that?

ALBOURY. The singing of toads. They call the rain.

LEONA. And that?

ALBOURY. The crying of hawks. (*Pause.*) And the sound of a motor.

LEONA. I don't hear a motor.

ALBOURY. I hear it.

LEONA. It sounds more like water.

ALBOURY. Did you hear?

LEONA. No.

ALBOURY. A dog.

LEONA. I don't think I hear it.

Barking of a dog in the distance.

It's just some harmless little runt. You can tell from the bark. It's just a puppy, and it's far away. I don't even hear it any more.

Barking of a dog in the distance.

ALBOURY. He is looking for me.

LEONA. Let him come. I love dogs, petting them. They don't attack if you like them.

ALBOURY. They are bad animals. They smell me from far away. They run after me and bite at me.

LEONA. Are you frightened?

ALBOURY. Yes, yes, I am frightened.

LEONA. Of a little runt we can't even hear any more!

ALBOURY. We frighten chickens; and dogs frighten us.

LEONA. I want to stay with you. What is there for me to do with them? I quit my job, I quit everything. I left Paris, aiyaiyaiee, I left everything. All I've been looking for is someone to be faithful to. I've found him. And now, I can't move from here. (*Closes her eyes.*) I think my heart has a devil in it, Alboury. How he got there, I'll never know, but he's there, I can feel him. He caresses me inside and I'm already burnt all black inside.

ALBOURY. Women are so fast to talk; I cannot keep up.

LEONA. Fast? You call this fast? When I haven't thought of anything else for at least an hour? After thinking about it for a whole hour, I can't say that it's serious, that I've thought it over, definitely? Tell me what you thought when you first saw me.

ALBOURY. I thought, a coin someone dropped in the sand; for now, she glitters for no one. So I can grab her up and keep her until somebody claims her.

LEONA. Keep her, nobody will claim her.

ALBOURY. The old man told me you were his.

LEONA. Cookie? Is he the one who's worrying you? For heaven's sake. He wouldn't hurt a flea, the poor thing.

Leave it to me, I'll take care of everything. What do you think I am to him? A little company, a little fling, because he has some money and doesn't know what to do with it. And for me who doesn't have any, aren't I lucky to have met him? If my mother knew, oh, she'd frown and say, 'You little tramp, that kind of thing only happens to actresses and prostitutes.' But I'm not either one and it happened to me. When he asked me to join him in Africa, I said yes, yes, I'm ready. '*Du verkörperst den Teufel, Schelmin!*'

Cookie's so old, so sweet. He never asks for anything, you know. That's why I like old men, and they like me, usually. They smile at me, in the street, I feel good, around them, I feel close to them, I feel their . . . vibrations. Can you feel vibrations from old people, Alboury?

Myself, sometimes, I just want to be old and sweet; chatting away for hours, not expecting anything from anybody, not asking anybody for anything, not being afraid of anything, not saying anything bad about anyone, far away from cruelty and unhappiness.

A faint noise, the cracking of a branch?

Everything is so calm, so sweet.

Cracking of branches, muffled calls in the distance.

It's so nice here.

ALBOURY. For you, yes, for me, no. This is a place for whites.

LEONA. A little longer, just one minute more. My feet hurt. These shoes are awful. They cut into your ankles and toes. Isn't this blood here? Look. This is a nice little mess. Three little bits of leather just made for you to wreck your feet in, and for this they charge you an arm and a leg. I don't really feel up to walking.

ALBOURY. That is too bad; I would have kept you as long as I could have.

Sound of a van nearby.

LEONA. He's coming.

ALBOURY. It is the white.

LEONA. He won't do anything to you.

ALBOURY. He is going to kill me.

LEONA. No!

They huddle together and hide. The van can be heard as it comes to a stop; the headlights light up the ground.

Scene Twelve

CAL, *with a rifle in his hand, covered with blackish mud.*

HORN (*emerges suddenly from out of the darkness*). Cal!

CAL. Boss? (*Laughs; runs toward him.*) Ah, boss, am I glad to see you, boss.

HORN (*making a face*). Where'd you crawl out of?

CAL. The shit, that's where.

HORN. Good god, don't come any closer, you'll make me throw up!

CAL. You're the one who told me to do whatever I had to to find him.

HORN. So? Did you?

CAL. Nothing, boss, nothing.

He cries.

HORN. So you got yourself all covered with shit for nothing! (*Laughs.*) Christ, what an idiot.

CAL. Don't make fun of me, boss. It was your idea, I always have to do everything by myself. It was your idea and I'm going to get lockjaw because of you.

HORN. Go back to camp. You're completely loaded.

CAL. No. No, boss. I want to find him, I have to find him.

HORN. Find him? It's too late now, you idiot. He's floating down some river somewhere by now. And it's going to rain. It's too late. (*Walks toward the van.*) The seats must be a goddamn mess. Jesus, it stinks!

CAL (*grabs HORN by the collar*). You're in charge, Horn, you're the boss. You're supposed to tell me what to do now. But you just watch it, you asshole, don't you make fun of me.

HORN. Remember your nerves, don't get all excited. Let's go, Cal. You know I'm not making fun of you.

CAL *lets go of him.*

So what happened? We're going to have to disinfect you now.

CAL. Look how I'm sweating, fucking shit, look at this, it'll never dry. Don't you have a beer? (*Cries.*) Don't you have any milk? I want a glass of milk, Horn.

HORN. Calm down. We'll go back to camp. You've got to get washed up and it's going to rain.

CAL. So can I get rid of him now, huh? Can I get rid of him now?

HORN. Not so loud, for God sake!

CAL. Horn!

HORN. What?

CAL. Am I really a son of a bitch, man?

HORN. What are you talking about?

CAL *cries.*

Cal, c'mon, son.

CAL. All of a sudden I saw Toubab standing in front of me, looking at me, thinking with his little eyes. Toubab, hey boy, what are you dreaming about, boy, what are you thinking about? Then he growls and the fur on his back stands up and he starts walking along the sewer, real careful. I follow him. Toubab, hey boy, what are you thinking about? You smell somebody? His fur stands up, he lets out a little bark and jumps into the sewer. 'He smelled somebody,' I say, and I followed him in. But I didn't find anything, boss. Just shit. But that's where I threw him in. He must have got out somehow. I can't search every stream and drag the lake looking for the body. And now Toubab's gone too. I'm all alone again, covered with shit. Horn!

HORN. What?

CAL. Why am I being punished? What did I do that was so bad?

HORN. You did what you were supposed to do.

CAL. So I can get rid of him, old man? Is that what I should do now?

HORN. Keep it down, damn it. You want the whole village to hear?

CAL (*Loads his gun*). This is a perfect spot. Nobody around to see anything, nobody to make complaints or come around crying. You'd just disappear into the bushes here. You bastard, your skin isn't worth shit here. I'm getting fired up again, man, I'm gettin' hot.

He starts sniffing around.

HORN. Give me that rifle.

He tries to grab it away from him; CAL *resists.*

CAL. Look out, man. I may not be good at karate and I may not be good at knives, but when it comes to guns, look out. Revolver, machine gun, you name it. You're not worth shit when I've got this.

HORN. You want the whole village on your back? You want to have to explain yourself to the police? You want to go on screwing things up. (*Low.*) Do you trust me? Do you trust me or not? So just let me handle this. Don't let your nerves get the best of you. You've got to stay cool. And by morning, everything'll be taken care of, believe me. I don't like blood, son, I don't like it at all. I've never gotten used to it. I can't take it. I'll talk to him one more time and this time everything will be taken care of, believe me. I've got a few little secret methods of my own. What good would spending all this time in Africa have been if I didn't? What's the good of bloodshed if things can just take care of themselves?

CAL (*sniffs*). I smell bushes that have eyes and ears. He's right here, boss, can't you smell him?

HORN. Cut the funny business.

CAL. Don't you hear it, boss?

Barking in the distance.

Is that him? Yes, yes, it is. Toubab! Here, boy, come here, don't ever leave me again, let me pet you, and stroke you . . . (*cries.*) I love him, Horn. Horn, why am I being punished, why am I such a son of a bitch?

HORN. You're not a son of a bitch.

CAL. Well you're an asshole, a fucking asshole, because I am a son of a bitch, I want to be, I decided to be one. All you can do is talk. Talk and more talk. And what are you going to do if he doesn't listen to you, huh? If your secret little methods don't work, huh? And they won't work either, goddammit, so you should be glad I'm a son of a bitch, that there's at least one of us who's got the balls to do it. When it comes to action you and your kind aren't worth a damn.

If one of these boubous spits at me, I shoot him, and I'm right, damn it. And it's thanks to me they don't spit on you and not because of all your . . . your talk or because you're an asshole. If he spits at me, he's a dead man, and you're glad he is because a little closer and it'd be on our feet and a little higher and it'd be on our pants, and a little higher than that and it'd be in our face. What would you have done if I hadn't done something? You'd just talk away with his spit dripping down your face. Fucking asshole!

They're always spitting around here. And what do you do? You pretend like you don't see it. They open one eye and spit, then the other and spit, they spit while they're walking, they spit while they're eating, and drinking, sitting, lying down, standing up, squatting, between every mouthful, between every swallow, every minute of the day. It covers the sand and the paths all around here. It seeps in and turns to mud and you walk in it and your boots sink down into it. And just what is spit made of? Can you tell me that? Liquid, like the body, ninety per cent. But what about the other ten per cent? Who's gonna tell me that, huh? You! Well I'll tell you one thing, all this boubou spit is gonna get you.

If you collected all the spit all the niggers in all the tribes all over Africa spit in just one day, if you dug wells for it, canals, dikes, locks, dams, aqueducts, if you joined all the rivers of spit the black race spits on this continent and on us, it would cover all the dry land on the planet with a sea that would threaten our lives. There wouldn't be anything but the oceans of salt water and the oceans of spit all mixed together and only the niggers would be left, floating in their own element. Well I'm not going to let it happen. I believe in doing something about it, so when you're through talking, Horn, when you're all through, Horn . . .

HORN. Let me do it my way first. If I can't convince him . . .

CAL. Ah hah, boss.

HORN. But calm down first, just calm your delicate nerves, for God sake.

CAL. Ah hah, boss.

HORN. Now look, Cal, be a good boy . . .

CAL. Shut up!

Barking in the distance; CAL runs off like a shot.

HORN. Cal! Come back! That's an order! Come back here!

The sound of a truck starting up. HORN doesn't move.

Scene Thirteen

Cracking of branches. HORN turns on his flashlight.

ALBOURY (*in the dark*). Put out the light.

HORN. Alboury?

Silence.

Come here, where I can see you.

ALBOURY. Put out your light.

HORN (*laughs*). Why so jumpy? (*Turns the flashlight off for a moment.*) You know your voice sounds a little scary.

ALBOURY. Show me what you are hiding behind your back.

HORN. Ah hah, behind my back, huh? Rifle? Revolver? Guess the caliber.

From behind his back he produces two bottles of whisky.

Ah hah! So this is what I'm hiding! You still doubt my intentions?

He laughs, turns the flashlight back on.

Come on, relax. I really want you to taste these. They're the best I've got.

Just remember that I've come one hundred per cent of the way to meet you, Alboury. You don't want to come to me, so, I come to you. And believe me, I do it out of friendship, pure friendship. But what can I do? You've managed to worry me, I mean, you've aroused my interest. (*Holds up the whisky.*) This'll help you loosen up a little. I forgot the glasses. I hope you're not a snob, besides, whisky's much better straight from the bottle, keeps it from going flat. That's how you can tell a real drinker. I want to teach you how to drink. (*Low.*) What's the matter, Alboury, guilty conscience?

ALBOURY. Why?

HORN. Oh, I don't know. It's just that your eyes keep moving all over the place.

ALBOURY. The other white is looking for me. And he has a rifle.

HORN. I know, I know. Why do you think I'm here? With me here, nothing's going to happen to you. Here, I hope you don't mind drinking from the same bottle.

ALBOURY drinks.

Give it time to go down; in a little while it'll give up its secret.

They drink.

So I understand you're some kind of karate ace. Is that right, are you a karate ace?

ALBOURY. That depends what that means – ace.

HORN. You never want to tell me anything! But I'd really like to learn one or two moves some day when we have some time. All the same, I want to tell you right now I don't put much stock in these oriental martial arts. Give me good old boxing! You ever done any good old-fashioned boxing?

ALBOURY. Old-fashioned, no.

HORN. Well, how do you expect to defend yourself then? I'll show you one or two punches, one of these days. I was real good too, I even boxed professionally, when I was young. Now that's an art you never forget. (*Low.*) Take it easy now, relax. You're here with me and as far as I'm concerned, hospitality is sacred. Besides, you're practically on French territory here. So you don't have anything to worry about.

They switch from one bottle to the other.

I'm curious to know which one you prefer. It tells you a lot about a man.

They drink.

This one here has a very definite sharpness to it; can you feel how sharp it is? While that other one is very smooth, it rolls; it's like thousands of little metal balls, little ball bearings, isn't it? How does it feel to you? Ah, no doubt about the sting in this one. And if you give it time, you can feel a tingling, a prickling sensation in your mouth, can't you? Well?

ALBOURY. I do not feel little balls or sting or tingling.

HORN. You don't? But there's no question. Try again. You're not afraid of getting drunk are you?

ALBOURY. I will stop before then.

HORN. Very good, good, excellent, bravo.

ALBOURY. Why did you come here?

HORN. To see you.

ALBOURY. To see me? Why?

HORN. To get a good look at you, to shoot the breeze, kill some time. To be friendly, that's all, just being friendly. And for a lot of other reasons too. You don't like my company? But you told me you enjoy learning new things, didn't you?

ALBOURY. I have nothing to learn from you.

HORN. Bravo. It's true. I had a feeling you were making fun of me.

ALBOURY. The only thing I've learned from you, in spite of you, is that there isn't enough room in your head and in all your pockets for all your lies. In the end, they all come to light.

HORN. Bravo. However, it's not true. Go ahead, try me. Ask me for anything you want, to prove I'm not lying to you.

ALBOURY. Give me a gun.

HORN. Except a gun. No. You're all going crazy with all your pop guns!

ALBOURY. He has one.

HORN. Too bad for him. Enough of that idiot. He'll end up behind bars and all the better. If somebody would take him off my hands, I'd be happy. I'll level with you, Alboury. He's the cause of all my problems. Get rid of him for me and I won't bat an eye. Now you level with me too, Alboury. What do your superiors intend to do?

ALBOURY. I have no superiors.

HORN. So then why are you acting like you're from the secret police?

ALBOURY. *Dommi xaram!*

HORN. Oh, so you want to go on playing cat and mouse. Have it your way.

ALBOURY *spits on the ground.*

Don't get mad about it.

ALBOURY. How could a man find his way through all your words and betrayals?

HORN. Look, Alboury, when I tell you do whatever you want with him, that I won't cover for him any more, I'm telling you the truth, believe me. I'm not playing around.

ALBOURY. It is a betrayal.

HORN. A betrayal? Of what? What are you talking about now?

ALBOURY. Your brother.

HORN. Oh no, please, spare me your African words. What that man does is none of my business, his life doesn't affect me in the least.

ALBOURY. But you are of the same race, aren't you? The same language? The same tribe?

HORN. The same tribe? Well, I guess you could say that, yes.

ALBOURY. Both of you are masters here, yes? Masters over opening and closing the projects, masters over hiring and firing the workers? The two of you are owners of the trucks and machines? The brick huts and the electricity, of everything here. The two of you, yes?

HORN. Yes, you could say that, roughly speaking, yes. So what?

ALBOURY. Why are you afraid of the word 'brother'?

HORN. Because things have changed a lot in the last twenty years, Alboury. And what's changed is the difference between him and me, between a greedy, crazed murderer on the loose, and a man who came here with a completely different attitude.

ALBOURY. I don't know what your attitude is.

HORN. I started out as a worker, Alboury. Believe me, I'm not a master by nature, you know. When I came here, I knew what it was to be a worker; and that's why I've always treated my workers, black or white, the same, like I was treated when I was a worker. The attitude I'm talking about is this: I know that if a worker is treated like an animal, he'll get revenge like an animal. That's the difference. And as for the rest of it, you're not going to blame me if the workers here are unhappy, like everywhere else. That's the way it is, there's not a damn thing I can do about it. I've been paid to know that. You don't by any chance believe there's a worker anywhere in the world who can say, 'I'm happy' do you? Besides, do you realily think there's a man anywhere in the world who'll ever say, 'I'm happy'?

ALBOURY. What do workers care about their master's feelings? And what do blacks care about the feeling of whites?

HORN. You're one tough customer, Alboury. I'm not a man to you, am I? Whatever I say, whatever I do, whatever idea I might have, even if I pour my heart out to you, you'd only see a white and a boss. (Pause.) What does it matter in the end? It doesn't keep us from drinking together.

They drink.

It's strange. You always seem to have your mind on something else, as if there was somebody behind you. You're so distracted. No, no, don't say anything. Just drink. Are you drunk already?

ALBOURY. No.

HORN. Very good, bravo! (Low.) I have a favour to ask you, Alboury. Don't say anything to her. Don't tell her what brought you here, don't tell her about any deaths or anything like that, don't say anything that might scare her away. I hope you haven't already. Maybe I shouldn't have brought her here, I know, but I just got it into my head, that's all. I know it's crazy but I couldn't get it out of my head, and now, I just don't want anything to scare her away. I need her, I need to feel her nearby. I hardly even know her, I don't know what she wants, but she can do as she pleases. It's enough for me just to have her around, and I'm not asking for anything else. Don't chase her away. (Laughs.) Look, Alboury, I don't want to end up all alone like some old fool. (Drinks.) I've seen a lot of dead people in my life and every time I see a dead person's eyes I tell myself, you've got to treat yourself to everything you want, right now, and you have to spend the money for it right away. If not, what's the use of having it? I don't have a family.

They drink.

Goes down good, doesn't it? You don't seem to be afraid of alcohol, that's good. You're not drunk yet? You're a tough one. Can I see?

He takes ALBOURY's *left hand.*

Why do you let this nail grow so long and not the others? (Contemplates the nail.) Is it some kind of religious thing? Is it a secret? (Feels it.) It must be a terrible weapon, if you know how to use it; a regular little dagger. (Lower). Or maybe it's for some sort of love-making? I'll tell you something, Alboury, once you start trusting women, you're lost! (Looks at him). But you're not talking, you're keeping all your secrets to yourself. I know that deep down, and right from the start, you've been laughing at me.

He suddenly takes a roll of bills out of his pocket and holds it out to ALBOURY.

Here you go, friend, like I promised. Five hundred dollars. It's all I can do.

ALBOURY. You promised me the body of Nouofia.

HORN. You're not going to start that again, are you? That's it – Nouofia. And didn't you tell me he had a secret name too? What was it again?

ALBOURY. It is the same, for all of us.

HORN. That does me a lot of good. What was it?

ALBOURY. I have told you: the same for all of us. It is not spoken otherwise. It is secret.

HORN. You're too deep for me. I like things to be nice and clear. Here, take it.

He holds out the roll of money.

ALBOURY. That's not what I want from you.

HORN. OK, so a worker is dead. It's serious, I agree, I don't want to minimize it, not at all. But it can happen anywhere, any time. Don't you think workers die in France? It's serious, but it happens. If it hadn't been him, it would have been somebody else. What do you expect? The work here is dangerous, all of us, we all take risks. Besides, it's all within limits. Let's be straight, OK? Work costs what it costs. Every society sacrifices part of itself, every person sacrifices a part of himself. That's what makes the world go round, huh, and you're not going to be the one to stop it now, are you? Don't be naïve, Alboury. You can be sad, I can understand that, but don't be naïve. (*Holds out the money.*) Here, take it.

ALBOURY *moves toward him menacingly.* HORN *draws back.* LEONA *enters.*

Scene Fourteen

Flashes of lightning, more and more frequent.

HORN. Leona, I was looking for you. It's going to rain and you don't know

what rain is like here. This'll just take me a minute and then we'll go back. (*Low; to* ALBOURY.) You're just too complicated for me, Alboury, that's all. Your thoughts are all jumbled together, like the bush out there, like Africa, like your whole continent. I wonder why I ever loved it so much. I wonder why I was so determined to save you. You'd think everybody here had gone crazy.

LEONA (*To* HORN). Why are you tormenting him?

HORN *looks at her.*

Give him what he's asking for. Give him that man's body.

HORN. Leona! (*Laughs.*) Good God, this is all getting very dramatic. (*To* ALBOURY.) Listen to me, nobody is ever going to find that worker's body. What's left of it, what hasn't been eaten by the fish or the birds by now, is floating down some river somewhere. So get it out of your head once and for all. (*To* LEONA.) It's going to rain, Leona, come on.

LEONA *moves closer to* ALBOURY.

ALBOURY. Get me a gun.

HORN. No, for god sake, no. I'm not going to let this place be turned into a slaughterhouse. (*Pause.*). Let's be reasonable. Leona, come here. Alboury, take this money and get out of here before it's too late.

ALBOURY. If I have lost Nouofia forever, then I will have the death of his murderer.

HORN. Thunder and lightning, mister; go settle things with the sky and get the hell out, go on, get out of here now. Leona, get over here!

LEONA *takes* ALBOURY *aside.*

Scene Fifteen

LEONA. Do what he says, Alboury, do it. He's even offering you money, money nicely, what more do you need? He came to settle things, that much is clear, and . . . well, you have to settle things when you can. What good is wanting to fight for something that doesn't mean anything any more when he's come nicely offering to settle things and money too? It's the other one who's crazy, but we know that now, we just have to watch out, and in the end, the three of us, we'll be able to keep him from messing up the whole works, I'm sure we can, from wrecking everything, and then things'll just roll right along.

But him, it's not the same thing at all; he came to talk to you nicely, but you, you say no, you clench your fists, you're being so stubborn, ooh! I've never seen anyone so stubborn. And you think that's how to get something? For heaven's sake, he just doesn't know how to go about it, not at all. But I know exactly how, if you'd let me. Certainly not by making fists and putting on all these belligerent airs and so stubborn, aiyaiyaiee.

I don't want to live with you at war, no, fighting's not what I want, or to be trembling all the time or unhappy, with you. I want to live, that's all, peacefully, in a little house, wherever you want, peaceful. Oh, I wouldn't even mind being poor, it doesn't matter to me, fetching the water and living off the trees, the whole kit and caboodle. I'm ready to live off absolutely nothing at all with you, but not to kill and fight, oh, no, why be so hard?

Or else I'm not worth a half-eaten dead man, I wouldn't be worth that much! Alboury, is it because I happened to be born white? But you can't make a mistake about me, Alboury. I'm not really a white, I'm not. I'm already so used to being what you shouldn't be; it doesn't cost me anything to be black on top of everything else. If that's it, Alboury, my whiteness, I already spit that out a long time ago, threw it out, I don't want it. So, if you, if you don't want me either . . .

Oh black, colour of all my dreams, colour of my love! I swear, when you go back to your home, I'll go with you; when I hear you say 'my home' I'll say 'my home'. To your brothers I'll say 'brothers', to your mother, 'mother'. Your village will be mine, your language will be mine, your land will be my land, and even in your sleep, I swear, even in your death, I'll still follow you.

HORN (*from a distance*). Can't you see he doesn't want anything to do with you? He's not even listening to you.

ALBOURY. *Démale falé, domou xatt bi!*

He spits in her face.

LEONA (*turns toward HORN*). Help me, help me.

HORN. What? You carry on with this guy, right under my nose, without the least bit of self-respect, and I'm supposed to help you? You think you can treat me like shit and I'm not going to react? You think all I'm good for is to shell out, to put out the money and then be treated like shit? Tomorrow, I swear to God, you're going back to Paris.

He takes a pistol out of his pocket.

As for you, my good man, I wouldn't want to be in your skin from now on. Where the hell do you think you are? I could have you shot like a common thief. You're damn lucky I don't like bloodshed. But I'll tell you something, you can cut the high and mighty act and start saying your prayers. Did you really think you could just come in here, take advantage of a French woman, right under my nose, on French property, without having to pay the consequences now? Get out of here. I'll let you explain things down in your village when they find out you tried to take advantage of a white woman and blackmail us. And I'll let you find your own way out of here without running into the other one who'd like nothing more than to have your skin. Go on, get out! And if anybody ever sees you inside this camp again, you'll be shot, by the police if necessary. I wash my hands of your filthy skin.

ALBOURY *disappears. Rain begins to fall.*

Scene Sixteen

HORN. As for you, spare me your little

scene now, please. It's the only thing that's missing. Oh no, no, I can't stand crying, it drives me out of my mind, stop it, please, have a little self-respect. You can hear everything here, the slightest noise travels for miles. We must be quite a sight, I swear, I wish you could see yourself. Shhh, come on now. Try to get a hold of yourself. Take a deep breath and hold it a minute, do whatever you want, take a swig of this, like you do for hiccups, it should work for this too, but just stop it. Here, take a drink.

He thrusts the bottle toward her.
LEONA *drinks.*

Have another, a big one. Where is Cal and that goddamn truck? Cal! Jesus Christ. Please, please! If you think that guy's not right around here somewhere, watching us, gloating over this pitiful little display. What a great image you give of the white race. Christ, where did I ever get such a big idea? Leona, please, I'm begging you, I can't take this kind of scene.

He walks around in all directions.

I feel bad, real bad.

He stops suddenly near LEONA. *Low and very quickly.*

Please, and what if . . . what if we left here, huh? what if I left the project right now, would . . . (*Takes her hand.*) Don't . . . don't cry any more . . . don't leave me alone. I have enough money to leave without giving notice and Cal could take over and in a couple of days we'd be in France, or Switzerland, or Italy, Lake Bolsena, Lake Constance, wherever you want. I've got the money. Don't cry, don't cry. Leona, with you I . . . Say it, say 'Yes'. Don't leave me, not now, I feel too bad now. Leona, I want to marry you, that's what we wanted, wasn't it? Say it, say 'Yes'.

LEONA *collects herself. She breaks the bottle of whiskey against a rock and suddenly, without a sound, staring into the shadows where* ALBOURY *has disappeared, using a shard of glass, she cuts deeply into her cheeks the scarifications resembling the tribal markings on* ALBOURY's *face.*)

HORN. Cal! Good God! Cal! She's bleeding. This is insane. Cal! There's blood all over!

LEONA *faints.* HORN *runs yelling toward a pair of approaching headlights.*

Scene Seventeen

On the verandah, near the table. CAL *cleans his rifle.*

CAL. I can't do anything, not in this light. Nothing. The guards would see me do it and they could be witnesses. They could run to the police and I don't want to have anything to do with the police. Or they could run to the village and I don't want to have the whole village on my back. I can't do a thing with all this light.

HORN. The guards won't do anything. They're too happy to have a job. Why would they run to the police or the village if they don't want to lose their jobs? They won't see anything; they won't hear anything; they won't do anything.

CAL. They already let him in once before, and now this time again. There he is again behind the tree. I can hear him breathing. I don't trust the guards.

HORN. Either they didn't see him come in or else they were sleeping. Besides, I haven't heard them for quite a while. They're sleeping. They won't do anything.

CAL. Sleeping? You don't see too well, do you? I can see them. They're looking right at us; they're watching us. That one there's scratching his leg; and that one just spit on the ground. There's no way I can do anything with all this light.

HORN (*after a pause.*). The generator's got to have some sort of breakdown.

CAL. Yeah, it does; it's got to, absolutely. If not, there's nothing I can do.

HORN. No, the best thing is to wait till morning. We'll send a radio call and the van to town. Well, I'm going to set up the mortars.

CAL. The what?

HORN. The launchers and the rockets, all the stuff for my fireworks.

CAL. But it's almost daybreak, Horn. Besides, she's shut up in the bungalow. She's not going to want to come out and watch them now, she didn't even want anybody to take care of her. If she comes down with lockjaw, we'll be stuck with her. She's one strange woman, and now she's got those marks for the rest of her life; and she was good-looking too. It's funny. And you . . . just who do you think is going to watch your fireworks?

HORN. Me, I'm going to watch them. I'm doing it for myself, I bought them for myself.

CAL. And what am I supposed to do? Let's stick together, man. We have to get rid of him once and for all.

HORN. I have faith in you. Just be careful, that's all.

CAL. But I've gone cold. I can't figure out how to do it.

HORN. One black skin is like every other black skin, right? The village wants a body, so we have to give them one. There won't be any peace around here till they get a body.

CAL. But they'll know right away it's not the worker. They can tell each other apart.

HORN. There are ways of fixing it so they can't tell. If you can't recognise the face, who's to say 'It's him' or 'It's not him?' The face, that's the only way to tell.

CAL (after a pause). I can't do anything without a rifle. I don't like to fight and besides these bastards are all too strong, them and their fucking karate. And with a rifle, they'll see the bullet hole in the face and then we'll all have the police on our backs.

HORN. So the best thing is to wait till morning. Let's play by the rules, son, that's the best thing to do. We'll talk with the police and settle things as best we can, by the rules.

CAL. Horn, I hear him, breathing, over there. What can I do? What should I

do? I can't think of anything. Don't leave me, Horn.

HORN. He could be run over by a truck. Who's to say it was a bullet or a lightning bolt or a truck that hit him, huh? A bullet hole doesn't look like anything if a truck runs over him afterwards.

CAL. Well, I'm going to bed. My head is killing me.

HORN. You idiot.

CAL (threatening). Don't call me an idiot, Horn, don't you ever call me an idiot again.

HORN. Cal, c'mon, son, remember your nerves. (Pause.) What I mean is, if you let this one go back to the village, two or three others'll come back, and then try to get rid of two or three! But if you don't, tomorrow we'll have his body carried to the village and tell them this is the one who was hit by lightning yesterday on the construction site and then, you see, a truck ran over him. Afterwards everything will be back to normal.

CAL. But then they'll ask us about this one. They'll ask us, 'What happened to the other one?'

HORN. This one's not a worker, we don't have to account for his whereabouts. Never saw him; don't know a thing. So?

CAL. It's hard to do it cold, just like that.

HORN. And when there's more of them, afterwards, when the guards start letting them all in, what're you going to do then, huh?

CAL. I don't know, I don't know. Tell me, old man.

HORN. It' better to get rid of the fox than to lecture the hen.

CAL. Yes, boss.

HORN. Besides, I already softened him up. He's not dangerous any more. He can barely stand up. He's been drinking like a fish.

CAL. Yes, boss.

HORN (low). Nice and careful, right in the face.

CAL. Yes.

HORN. And then the truck, nice and careful.

CAL. Yes.

HORN. Careful, careful, real careful.

CAL. Yes, boss, yes.

HORN. Cal, listen, son, you see I've decided not to stay till the project closes.

CAL. Boss!

HORN. Yes, son, that's how it is. I've had it. I don't understand anything about Africa any more. There must be another way, but I don't understand anything any more.

When the time comes for you to wind things up, Cal, damn it, listen to me! Don't hide anything from the management. Don't try to pull off any of your tricks. Tell 'em everything, everything. The police too, you just don't know them. Let them talk to the company. The people who run your company, they're the only thing that exists for you. Always remember that.

CAL. Yes, boss.

HORN. It'll be daybreak in a couple of hours. I'm going to start my fireworks.

CAL. What about her?

HORN. She'll be leaving with the van in a little while. I don't want to hear anything more about her. She never existed. We're all alone here. So long.

CAL. Horn!

HORN. What?

CAL. There's too much light, way too much.

HORN *looks up toward the watchtowers and the motionless guards.*

Scene Eighteen

In front of the half-open door of the bungalow.

HORN. A van will be leaving, in a few hours, to take some papers into town. It'll honk; be ready. He's a good driver. Meantime, it'd be dangerous for you to come out. Shut yourself in your room and don't move, no matter what you hear, until the van honks. By the time you leave, I'll already be at work, so goodbye. See a doctor when you get back. I hope he can fix all that up for you. Yeah, maybe a good doctor can make you presentable again and fix all that up. And when you get back, I'd also appreciate it if you wouldn't say too much. Think whatever you want, but don't say anything that'll hurt the company. It's not responsible for what happened to you. I'm asking you this as a . . . as a favor. I gave it everything, everything; it means everything to me. Think whatever you want about me, but don't do anything that'd hurt the company, because I'd be responsible, it'd be my fault. That's one favour *you* can do for *me*; since it's my money that bought the plane ticket that's getting you back. You took the ticket one way, now you've got to take it the other. So then . . . Goodbye. I'll never see you again. We'll never see each other again.

He exits.

LEONA *appears in the doorway, suitcases in hand. Her face is still bleeding. Suddenly the lights go out for a few seconds, then the generator can be heard starting up again.*
CAL *appears.* LEONA *hides her face with her arm and stays like that the entire time he talks to her.*
The lights flicker a few more times, interrupting CAL *now and then.*

Scene Nineteen

CAL. Take it easy, take it easy, babe, it's just the generator. Those big motors aren't easy to handle. I'd say we're about to have a blackout, it happens. Horn's probably taking care of it right now. Take it easy. (*Walks up to her.*) I washed up. (*Sniffs.*) I don't think I smell any more. I splashed on some aftershave. Do I still smell? (*Silence*). Poor baby, finding another job, now, I imagine, won't be too easy, will it? Especially in Paris, damn. It must be snowing in Paris now, huh? You're smart to go back. Besides, I knew it. I knew he'd end up disgusting you. I still don't know what you ever saw in Horn. When I first saw you, with your face all flushed, I mean red! So elegant, so chic you Paris women, always up on the latest fashions, so delicate! And when I look at you now . . . Horn is such an asshole! But anyway, for those of us who work here, you brought a little humanity to the place. And when you come right down to it, I can understand the old man, Horn, the old dreamer. (*Takes her hand.*) In any case, I'm glad I met you, I'm glad you came. I know you think I'm bad. I don't have any illusions. But what does it matter what you think of me, since you're going back to Paris, and we won't ever see each other again? I know you'll tell your friends bad things about me, for a while anyhow, and I know that as long as you do remember me, what you remember will be bad, and that, in the end, you won't remember me at all. Anyway, it's been nice talking to you. (*Kisses her hand.*) When will we ever see a woman around here again, a real woman like you? have a little fun with a woman, huh? when will I ever see a woman in this hell-hole again? I'm wasting what would be the best years of my life anyplace else. When you're alone, all the time, you end up forgetting your own age. Seeing you has helped me remember. I'll have to forget all over again. What am I here? Nothing. All this for money, babe. Money robs us of everything, even the memory of how old we are. Look. (*Shows her his hands.*) Would you still say these are the hands of a young man? Have you ever seen an engineer's hands in France? But what good is being young without money, huh? I really wonder why I'm alive.

The lights go out, this time for good.

Take it easy. It's just a blackout. Don't move. I've gotta go now. So long, babe. (*Pause.*) Don't forget me, don't forget me.

Scene Twenty

FINAL VISIONS OF A DISTANT ENCLOSURE

A first luminous explosion, silent and brief, in the sky above the bougainvillaea.

Blue flash from the barrel of a rifle. Dull sound of naked feet running on stone. Yelping of a dog. Glimmer of a flashlight. Someone whistles a short tune. Sound of a rifle being loaded. A fresh breeze rises.

The horizon is filled by an immense sunlike burst of colours that rain down, with a soft, muffled sound, in flakes of fire, on the camp.

Suddenly, the voice of ALBOURY: *a call rises up out of the blackness, warlike and secret, which turns, carried by the wind, and rises up out of the clump of trees to the barbed wire fences and from the fences to the watchtowers.*

Illuminated by the intermittent glow of the fireworks, accompanied by muted detonations, CAL *moves toward* ALBOURY's *motionless figure.* CAL *raises his rifle and aims at the head: sweat runs down his forehead and cheeks, his eyes red, filled with blood*

From out of the darkness, between explosions, an unintelligible dialogue between ALBOURY *and the heights surrounding him – a calm, indifferent conversation; brief questions and responses; laughter; indecipherable language which echoes and grows louder, running along the barbed wire, up and down, filling the entire area, reigning over the darkness and echoing over the entire petrified camp, in a final series of sparks and suns exploding in the sky.*

The first shot hits CAL *in the arm; he drops his rifle. Up in one of the towers, a guard lowers his gun; on another side, another guard raises his.* CAL *is hit in the stomach, then in the head; he falls.* ALBOURY *has disappeared. Blackness.*

The first faint signs of daybreak. Cries of a hawk in the sky. On the surface of the open sewer empty whisky bottles clink against each other. Honking of a horn. The flowers of the bougainvillaea sway, reflecting the light of dawn.

LEONA (*far off, her voice barely audible, covered by the sounds of the day; she leans toward the driver*). *Haben Sie ein* safety-pin? *Mein Kleid bindet sich los. Mein Gott,* if you don't have a safety-pin, *bin ich gezwungen nach Paris ganz entblösst* (Laughs, gets in the truck.) completely naked! *zurück kehren.*

The van drives off.

Next to CAL's *body – the shattered skull covered by the body of a white puppy, with its teeth bared.* HORN, *picks up the rifle, wipes his forehead and raises his eyes toward the deserted watchtowers.*

THESE CHILDISH THINGS

A Monodrama

Translated by Brian Singleton

Enfantillages was first presented at the Avignon Festival on 15 July 1984.

The play was performed by the author.

Directed by Raymond Cousse, with the collaboration of Christian Le Guillochet
Designed by Jean Herbin and Pierre Didelot
Costume by Claudine Sergent

Extracts of this translation were first read on 6 October 1987 at the French Institute in Edinburgh on the occasion of the British tour of *Enfantillages*.

RAYMOND COUSSE, praised by Beckett as 'an author of unquestionable talent', has written three full-length dramatic monologues, all of which he performs himself: *Stratégie pour deux jambons (Strategy for Two Hams)*, first produced at the Lucernaire Centre for Contemporary Theatre in Paris in 1979, *Enfantillages* (*These Childish Things*), premièred at the Avignon Theatre Festival in 1984 and *Le Bâton de la Maréchale*, which will be presented during the 1988/9 season. *These Childish Things* is a dramatic monologue which, like *Strategy for Two Hams*, has been performed in a wide variety of different venues.

DIRECTIONS

The play may be performed with or without a set. If it is then a pseudo-naïve village set.

The box is essential. Dimensions: 0.9 × 0.5 × 0.25m — mounted on wheels, with a rope and a handle. It suggests both the cradle and the coffin.

Child's country costume: short trousers, short-sleeved shirt and ankle socks.

An adult actor plays the role of the child. Maintain the distance between the two. In other words, don't resort to babyish behaviour. When the child is speaking to grown-ups, he looks upwards. This is reversed when a grown-up is speaking to children.

Narrate, visualize, mime; three levels of performance to be combined harmoniously. The musical unity of the text is the determining factor. The secondary characters originate from the leading character, that is from a childish point of view. Don't lapse into psychology.

The action is syncretic in nature. The play is anti-realistic, metaphysical. A simple succession of snapshots between life and death. Language forms a flimsy bridge between the two.

Scene One: Prologue

Dim light. The box is situated upstage centre. The actor enters left (in relation to the audience), skipping. Circles the stage and sits down on the box, facing the audience. Pause. Speaks softly

And I lay down on the bench with my grey coat to not catch cold saying to myself let's try

Pause. Like a naughty boy

Let's try to play dead

Lies down on the box, hands together, legs stretched out

Let's try I lay down on the bench saying to myself that's it I'm dead

Long pause. Keeps the pose, eyes closed

I'm dead like I'd seen in books on television in the newspapers war everywhere in the films in the cinema

Sits up gradually, facing right

Dead like in the hearses which passed by our house on Thursdays and everyday during the holidays sometimes two times a day except Sundays

Swivels round to face audience

On Sundays the hearses never passed by our house

He visualizes the scene

They passed by all the other days with their horses all in black with their coach all in black with the people all bent over following behind all in black too

Pause

With the people following

Gets up. Visualizing

Following behind with their walking-sticks and their hats all in black with their coats all in black with their gloves all in black too but never saying anything walking eyes down you would have said they were crying I do believe they were crying

Moves one step forward

They were crying but not all of them anyway I saw it

Visualizing

I saw it one day they told me to go up and do my homework they always told me to go up and do my homework when the hearses were passing by our house but I never did my homework I always looked out through the curtains and one day I was looking out through the curtains I saw it all

Pause

I saw that not all of them were crying

Moves one step forward. Visualizing

Not all of them but only some in the front row two or three and behind them a lot fewer and behind them even fewer still and behind them not at all

Pause. Resumes

Not all of them were crying.

Returns to the box, skipping

Scene Two: In the Butcher's

Harsh light. Circles the stage, dragging the box by the rope. Childish walk. Stops the

box downstage left. Sets it upright. It represents the door to the yard then to the butcher's, etc. During the scene, the action revolves around this central point. Points to the box

Let's try I was trying like I'd seen in the butcher's yard the cows the cattle the sheep stretched out in the butcher's yard even the little calves

Moves to the box

I was watching behind the lock standing on a brick and Marcel was watching too behind the lock standing on a brick me and Marcel were watching behind the lock standing on a brick we were watching and we saw

Behind the box. Visualizing and miming the scene

We saw the butcher in the butcher's yard with his apron and his white butcher's hat go up to the cows the cattle the sheep singing with his cleaver his knives and his butcher's pistol

Gestures sparingly

He goes up stroking their foreheads just a little between the horns Good boy nice little beastie nice little beastie even the little calves

Comes to life

But all of a sudden he could never help it he always got angry he stopped singing he shouted he raised his cleaver and his knives and he gave them one good shot in the head with his butcher's pistol in the yard

Moves back. Stunned

One good shot and bang the cows the cattle the sheep all tumbled to the ground flat on their backs even the little calves I was really sad then and I said to myself

Pause. Hesitates

I said to myself I said to myself what did I say to myself there you are I don't even know any more what I said to myself or if I did say to myself but I was sad all the same and I said to myself

Composes himself and goes back downstage. Moves to box

I was sad and Marcel was sad too me and Marcel were sad the pair of us but we fought all the same in the street to stand

on the brick to see into the yard to know how it would all end in the yard

Growing anxiety, flees upstage

We fought in the street but the butcher heard us in the yard he was angry in the yard he came chasing out after us running out after us with his cleaver his knives and his pistol

Retraces his steps, composes himself

He came chasing out after us but I could run faster than him and Marcel could run faster than him too he could never catch up with us and even suppose he had caught up with us he wouldn't have hit us in the street with his cleaver or his knives or even with his pistol it was only for fun

Bragging

It was only for fun the butcher had told my father and my father had told Marcel's father and Marcel's father had told my mother and then my mother had told me and then I had told Marcel

Goes on

Everyone knew that it was only for fun except the butcher I didn't tell the butcher we knew it was only for fun the butcher didn't know that we knew it was only for fun

Pause. Peers at audience argumentatively

But even if the butcher had known and even suppose he had hit us all the same with his pistol or his knives in the belly suppose or in the head or in the eye my father wouldn't have been happy

Visualizing the scene

He would have said to me serves you right that'll teach you but he wouldn't have been happy

Goes on

And Marcel's father wouldn't have been happy either he would have said to Marcel serves you right that'll teach you too but he wouldn't have been happy

Swivels round to the box – left side

My father and Marcel's father weren't happy the pair of them went into the butcher's

Behind the box, swivelling right

The butcher was waiting for them in the

butcher's What can I get you gentlemen
with his knives

Swivelling left. Naïvely

They would have said Well now we're
not happy why did you kill them in the
street with your knives it's not right at all

Comes to life

And perhaps they would have said If you
carry on like this we won't get our meat
from you any more that'll teach you.

Runs right. Aside

That'll teach you like once me and
Marcel heard in the butcher's that'll teach
you it was the village policeman's wife
talking to the butcher

Swivels right, shouts loudly

I'm not happy why did you kill my dog
I'll not get my meat from you anymore
that'll teach you you moron

Swivels left, mimes

But the butcher wasn't happy I didn't kill
your dog you fat sow

*Swivels to audience, visualizing the
scene*

He said he kept dogs and cats and even
guinea-pigs at home but he had never
killed his dogs or his cats let alone his
guinea-pigs his wife wouldn't let him

Continues

He said he even had flies at home but he
had never killed any of them either
except sometimes when they landed on
the meat he couldn't do anything else he
just swatted them once or twice

Walks to and fro downstage

But the village policeman's wife wasn't
happy she shouted she left she came back
she shouted again she came back again

Aside, childishly

But for several days she never got her
meat from the butcher's for fear of the
butcher playing a trick on her or of him
giving her suppose her dog to eat instead
of a steak everyone would have made fun
of her everyone would have had a good
laugh

Pause. Laughing

Me and Marcel laughed we said it's like
Old Mother Hubbard with her dog and

the Bogeyman with his fresh eggs

Faintheartedly, pointing upstage

Old Mother Hubbard went to the
cupboard to fetch her poor doggie it was
the Bogeyman who had stolen it he had
taken it home in his satchel to cook it in
his pot with his fresh eggs

Continues, visualizing the scene

But Old Mother Hubbard had seen the
Bogeyman put her doggie in his satchel
she tears down the stairs and there she is
running after the Bogeyman

Disgusted

She's running a really ugly old lady half
bald with rotten teeth varicose veins and
a bun

*Swivels round facing upstage. High-
pitched voice deforming the words*

She's running she's shouting Mister
Bogeyman give me back my doggie or I'll
tell Old Father Hubbard on you

Facing front

Old Father Hubbard is the husband of
Old Mother Hubbard he is the village
policeman at the town hall with his
helmet his notebook and pencil

Runs back, visualizes

But the Bogeyman had already put her
doggie in his pot with his fresh eggs he
lights the gas ring

High-pitched voice

Mother Hubbard shouts Mister
Bogeyman give me back my doggie or
Old Father Hubbard will put you in
prison

Aside

That's to make him afraid but the
Bogeyman isn't afraid.

Coarse and gravelly voice

Not so fast my dear give me a kiss or I'll
make a stew of your mutt

Long noisy kiss

Mother Hubbard kisses the Bogeyman on
the cheek with her rotten teeth

Comes to life

But the Bogeyman isn't happy he really
wants Old Mother Hubbard to kiss him
on the lips

Confidentially

But then Old Mother Hubbard can't kiss the Bogeyman on the lips she's married

High-pitched voice

She tells him I can't dear Mister Bogeyman I'm married

Aside

The Bogeyman isn't happy but he gives her back her doggie all the same

Coarse voice

Who cares I'm a decent chap

Runs upstage, mimes

He takes the doggie out of the pot by the tail but it's too late the doggie is already half cooked the Bogeyman bursts out laughing he can't stop laughing he slaps his thighs

Coarse voice

That's a good one that's a good one

Downstage, comes to life

But Old Mother Hubbard isn't laughing she's shouting she can't stop shouting at the Bogeyman

Gestures sparingly

Like the village policeman wife who couldn't stop shouting either in the butcher's

Pause. Continues

Who couldn't stop shouting in the butcher's the village policeman's wife couldn't stop shouting either in the butcher's

Calmly

But she didn't kiss the butcher the butcher would never have allowed the village policeman's wife to kiss him in the butcher's because of the butcher's wife who would have lost her temper behind her counter and because of the village policeman who would have lost his temper in the street

Swivels towards box military style

He would have gone into the butcher's In the name of the law stop fooling around

Visualizing

He would have summonsed the butcher

or he would have jumped over the counter and kissed the butcher's wife on the lips

Continues

But then his wife had seen him she lost her temper in the butcher's she was shouting even louder than she did her doggie

Lowering his voice

The butcher lost his temper too he was shouting even louder than about the village policeman's wife's doggie

Runs to centre

They were shouting and lost their temper all four of them in the butcher's

Clarifies

The butcher at the butcher's wife and the village policeman for the village policeman kissing the butcher's wife and at the village policeman's wife for her doggie

With panache

The butcher's wife at the butcher and the village policeman's wife for the village policeman's wife kissing the butcher and at the village policeman for kissing her behind the counter

Disoriented at the end

The village policeman at the butcher for his dog and at the butcher for kissing his wife at his wife for his wife kissing the butcher and at the butcher's wife for it's anyone's guess

Masterfully

Finally the village policeman's wife at the village policeman and the butcher's wife for the village policeman kissing the butcher's wife and at the butcher for her doggie

Beginning again

They lost their temper all four of them in the butcher's

Continues

The butcher was sharpening his knives The village policeman was sharpening his pencil

Visualizing

They were rolling on the floor all four of them in the butcher's

Continues

Me and Marcel could hear the shouting
but we couldn't see anything anymore

*Stamps his foot and peers out from
behind the box*

We watched we wondered who is going
to win

Stands up heavily behind the box, waits

But all of a sudden it was the butcher
who stood up in the butcher's he put his
hat back on his butcher's head he raised
his arms he cheered he had won

Counting on his fingers

He had killed his wife the village
policeman's wife and the village
policeman with his cleaver his knives and
his butcher's pistol

Comes out from behind box, mimes

He stood up he cheered he had won.

Continues

But all of a sudden he got angry again he
also killed his dogs his cats his guinea-
pigs and the flies in the butcher's

Hallucinating

And to finish with he got even angrier he
also killed his meat with his cleaver on
the counter in the butcher's

Saluting, arms in the air

It was the butcher who had won

*Keeps the pose. Suddenly adopts child's
pose*

Scene Three: Marcel's Sister

*He brings the box down, circling the
stage, dragging it by the rope. He brings it
to rest upstage right and sets it upright as
before. It represents the bedroom door.
Action revolves around this central point.
Points to box*

Flat on her back behind the lock but it
wasn't the lock on the door to the yard of
the butcher's anymore it was the lock on
the door to the bedroom of Marcel's
sister.

Gestures sparingly

It wasn't the cows the cattle the sheep
anymore it was Marcel's sister laid out on
her bed flat on her back with a hairy
beastie between her legs

Incredulous

A hairy beastie between her legs fancy
that me and Marcel had never seen a
hairy beastie before between his sister's
legs

Moves to box

We kept on watching behind the lock we
kept on listening there was someone

Aghast

There was someone in Marcel's sister's
bedroom with Marcel's sister it wasn't the
butcher it was his apprentice

Stunned

His apprentice fancy that Marcel's sister
was saying to him flat on her back come
this way my pet

Timidly moves away

I really didn't like Marcel's sister saying
to the butcher's apprentice come this way
my pet

Moves forward. Aside

But the butcher's apprentice did all the
same come this way my pet to stroke
Marcel's sister's hairy beastie.

Grotesque, miming

He did come but first he took off his hat
his boots and his apprentice butcher's
apron

Continues

He took off his trousers his braces his
flannel belt and his underpants my pet

Boyishly

The butcher's apprentice took off
everything behind the lock but he kept
on his watch and his socks then he
jumped on the bed with his watch and his
socks and his apprentice butcher's willy
three sizes bigger than the Senior school
boys

Visualizing

The butcher's apprentice jumped on the
bed and he stroked Marcel's sister's hairy
beastie and Marcel's sister stroked the
apprentice butcher's willy

Tenderly

They both stroked each other behind the

lock saying nice things to each other Nice little beastie and come this way my pet

Continues

But all of a sudden the butcher's apprentice got angry and jumped between Marcel's sister's legs flat on her back and beat the hairy beastie with his willy

Stunned

Marcel's sister was shouting but the butcher's apprentice was shouting too

Becoming sad

Me and Marcel heard the shouting but we couldn't see anything more

Goes to the box and visualizes

We could only see the butcher's apprentice's huge bum rise and fall and never stop behind the lock

Terrified. He moves away from the box. Confidentially

Come this way my pet I really didn't like Marcel's sister say to the butcher's apprentice come this way my pet

Timidly

She often said to me Come this way my pet when me and Marcel were drinking lemonade in the kitchen

Visualizing

We were drinking quietly when all of a sudden who should come into the kitchen only Marcel's sister and say to me Come this way my pet for a sweet or a chocolate cigarette

Backs away timidly

I didn't like that at all I always wanted to tell her

Childish anger

Take your hairy beastie away from me and don't call me my pet I don't like it at all

Aside, composes himself

I always wanted to but I never could for suppose I had spoken to her about the hairy beastie in the kitchen she would have known that me and Marcel had seen her hairy beastie in the bedroom behind the lock and we're not allowed

Points to the box

I didn't like it at all I was always afraid of her taking me off into her bedroom one day to have a drink of lemonade

Visualizing

We were drinking quietly when all of a sudden who should come into the kitchen only Marcel's sister and say to me Leave your lemonade my pet and come this way to my bedroom suppose I show you some nice colour postcards I'm sure you'll like them

Playful

Me and Marcel were very happy we really like looking at nice colour postcards

Runs to the box

We climb the stairs straightaway with the glass and the bottle

Stops. Suddenly worried

But then Marcel's sister turns round and says to Marcel No need you've already seen them go back down and drink your lemonade

Growing fear

But she says to me But you my pet have never seen them

Hauls himself with force behind the box

She takes me off into her room by the throat my pet and locks her bedroom door

Behind the box. Aside

I really don't like the doors locked when I'm being shown nice colour postcards

Sits down, snuggles up to the box terrified, peering out furtively

I hid myself in a corner but Marcel's sister didn't show me anything at all she only lay down on her bed flat on her back

Impatiently, raises the tone

I ask her Well where are your colour postcards then

Confidentially

Marcel's sister doesn't answer she only says Come this way my pet I'll show you something much nicer than colour postcards I'm sure you'll like it

Candidly

I didn't know anything nicer than colour postcards but Marcel's sister shows me her hairy beastie Come this way my pet I'm sure this is much nicer than postcards

Swallowing his saliva

I pretended I didn't understand I ask her again gulping

Snivelling, raises the tone

Well where are your colour postcards then

Increasing anxiety

But then Marcel's sister gets angry on her bed

Detached

Is there nothing else to life than postcards wally

Confidentially

She wants me to say no there's your hairy beastie as well

Moves away from box as he continues

I say No there's lemonade as well me and Marcel really like drinking lemonade we get it at the grocer's in exchange for the empty litre bottles with stars because the grocer never takes empty litre bottles without stars for three empty litre bottles you get a full litre bottle and if you want two full litre bottles you need six empty litre bottles with stars and for three full litre bottles you need nine empty litre bottles with stars and if you happen to be very thirsty and you want four full litre bottles you need

Gives a start

But then Marcel's sister gets even angrier on her bed

Detached

Are you trying to tell me you've got nothing between your legs wally

Terrorized

I say to myself that's it she knows I've got a willy she'll want to stroke it

Covers his crotch with his hands protectively

I'm trembling I'm very frightened in my corner with my willy six sizes smaller than the butcher's apprentice's

Composes himself

But all of a sudden I notice a suitcase under her bed

Pathetically

Wait I'll look see if your colour postcards could have fallen under your bed at some time

Flees on all fours. Mimes

I dive under the bed into the suitcase but the hairy beastie dives too it wants to catch my willy in the suitcase

On his knees. Protects his crotch with one hand, fighting with the other

Go away you dirty beastie there's no colour postcards here

Visualizing

I give it a good kick then I lock it in the suitcase

Relieved

And I go down quietly and drink my lemonade with Marcel in the kitchen

Goes back to the box in a bad mood

Scene Four: Big Boys' Willies

Drags the box upstage left, sets it upright, one side facing the audience. It represents the door to the toilets. Hesitates for a long time, makes up his mind, moves downstage. Confidentially

Three sizes bigger than the Senior school boys' we had never seen a willy three sizes bigger than the Senior school boys'

Bragging

But me and Marcel had seen willies one size bigger than the Senior school boys' when we went to stroke them with our hands in the toilets

Becoming sad

Because of the teacher who would never have allowed us to stroke the big boys' willies in the playground

Playful

The big boys really liked us to stroke their willies with our hands in the toilets they were very happy they gave us sweets and sometimes even cigarettes

Candidly

That was when they were even happier when me and Marcel had stroked their willies with our tongues in the toilets

Playful

They were even happier they gave us cigarettes

Becoming sad

But we could never smoke them in the toilets

Kneeling in front of the box, demonstratively

Because of the smoke that would have drifted out through the lock on the toilet door because of the teacher who would have seen the smoke drift out

Gets up, visualizing

He ran into the playground he blew his whistle he opened the toilet door he saw me and Marcel smoking he blew his top in the toilets

Swivels to the box

Smoking is not allowed why are you smoking

Swivels to the audience then right. Naïvely

Me and Marcel said to him We're smoking because the big boys gave us smoking cigarettes so we're smoking them

Swivels to audience

But the teacher blew his top even more in the toilets

To the box

And may I ask why the big boys gave you cigarettes

To the audience

The big boys gave us smoking cigarettes because they were very happy

To the audience

But the teacher wasn't happy

To the box

And may I ask why the big boys were very happy

To the right

The big boys were very happy because we stroked their willies with our tongues

in the toilets they were very happy they gave us smoking cigarettes to smoke so we're smoking them so there

To the audience, coming to life

But the teacher blew his top even more in the toilets he shouted he roared he turned all red in the toilets Me and Marcel said to him

To the right, calmly

You mustn't blow your top in the toilets

Moves forward

We said to him

To the right, deceitfully

We didn't know it wasn't allowed to smoke in the toilets next time we won't smoke in the toilets

Moves forward

We said to him

To the right, growing in confidence

Next time we won't stroke the big boys' willies with our tongues in the toilets only with our hands then they'll only give us sweets we're not allowed to smoke but we are allowed to eat sweets

To the audience, in triumph

Next time we'll eat sweets

Goes back to box, skipping

Scene Five: The Teacher

Pulls the box down, circles the stage, dragging the box by the rope. Sets it upright centre stage. It represents the teacher's desk. Stands to the right of the box, a little downstage

When me and Marcel went to school for the first time with the satchel

Squats, mimes

We were playing happily in the sand in the playground we were filling the satchel with shells it was nearly full by then

Jumps up, points at box

But all of a sudden there was the teacher blowing his whistle on the steps

Gets up. Teacher's stiff pose

Boys get yourselves into rows of two and keep in line

Relaxes and visualizes

Me and Marcel got ourselves into a row of two the pair of us we were still playing around a bit in line but the teacher wasn't playing around on the steps

Teacher's pose

Boys we've not come here to play around from now on you will not play around in your rows if you want to grow up to be men and serve your Country but first does everyone want to grow up to be a man

Relaxes

Everyone in unison says Yes

Teacher's pose

But first does everyone want to serve his Country

Relaxes

Everyone in unison again says Yes

Bragging, aside

Except me and Marcel me and Marcel said yes all the same but all the same we were thinking no because our Country we didn't know what our Country was

Teacher's pose

But the teacher shows us a lady in a picture on a wall with a stick that's our Country

Relaxes, aside

Marcel says to me Do you think she's got a hairy beastie too

Teacher's pose

But the teacher sees us talking again Obviously those two just can't stop ˙talking

Mimes

˙First of all give me that satchel what's in the satchel well look shells well now boys you are not allowed to fill your satchels with your Country's shells why have you filled your satchel nearly full with your Country's shells

Snivelling

Me and Marcel said to him we thought our Country's shells belonged to everyone and to us as well that's why we wanted to fill our satchel with our Count. . .

Teacher's pose

But the teacher sees us again Obviously those two just can't stop talking if you go on like this I'll be forced to separate you

Aside

Me and Marcel didn't talk anymore in our rows not because we didn't want to talk but because we didn't want the teacher to separate us

Skirts around the box, runs downstage left

We didn't talk anymore in our rows but we didn't talk anymore in class either because the teacher had said to us

Teacher's pose

Boys sit down in line and from now on no more talking in class either if you want to grow up to be men and serve your Country

Relaxes and visualizes

No one talked in class anymore everyone sat down in line the teacher in line too but higher up behind his desk

Goes behind the box, bends his knees and mimes a sitting position

Now fold your arms boys and be quiet once more be a bit quieter boys

Smoothly

Now I'm going to ask you a very easy question boys think about it then answer but careful not all at once

Moves off left, mimes

Not all at once careful the teacher showed us how not all at once elbows on the table hands in the air heels together but not too close no clicking of heels fingers or teeth you must wait your turn

Upright behind the box

A bit quieter again boys

'Sitting' position

Now here's the question boys ready I'll count to three one two three here's the question boys it's very easy what have you come here to do answer

Moves abruptly left

What have you come here to do boys fancy that no one answered no one knew what we had come here to do boys but the teacher said

'Sitting' behind the box

Come along boys it's very easy I'm going to help you you have come here to do three things first of all here to come along answer

Gets up. Hand raised, mimes

A voice in the class someone says To sleep

Reacts strongly

To sleep no nought out of ten I'm marking you haven't come here to sleep boys you have come here to come along here to secondly I'm listening

Hand raised, mimes

A voice in the class someone says To eat

Reacts strongly, 'sits down' again

To eat fancy that why not to drink while we're at it nought out of ten one hundred lines I'm marking no you haven't come here to eat you have come here to come along liven up boys here to thirdly

Hand raised, mimes

A voice in the class someone says To drink

Exhausted

To drink for God's sake I knew it to drink you young whelps boys now I've heard everything to drink just you wait you young drunks nought out of ten two hundred lines three verbs to conjugate I'm marking no you haven't come here to drink boys you've come here to come along answer

Furious, gets up.

Here to once here to twice here to three times answer immediately or I'll wallop you

Swiftly moves off right. Aside

Answer answer no one answered no one knew what we had come here to do or why or how except a boy repeating a class in the corner no one was listening to him except the teacher

Repeater's servility and growing satisfaction of the teacher. Mimes

Here first of all to learn to read
Well done boy one gold star
And to write

Well done boy two gold stars there's hope for you
And to count
Well done boy three gold stars keep your heels together
And to sing

Astonishment then anger

No not to sing you haven't come here to learn to sing useless absolutely useless two noughts out of ten three hundred lines four verbs to conjugate I take back the three gold stars let's go on

Aside

The teacher went on

Paces downstage. Smugly

Boys I'm going to have to tell you something you won't be too happy about and might even upset you I hope I have to tell you boys that never in my whole career serving my Country have I seen boys as ignorant as you

Returns behind the box, 'sits down'. Solemnly

Well anyway boys let's be reasonable about this I understand fine well that you can't know everything in one go and besides we all know the world we live in so vast and so beautiful wasn't created in a day but all the same there is a difference between that and not knowing where you're going when you go and especially why you're going and that's going too far I think you go too far boys well anyway

Gets up, paces again downstage then returns behind the box

Well anyway there are two things to choose from one is boys let's be reasonable either you know where you're going when you go and why you're going and if you do great or else you don't know at all and if this is the case I don't see why you go there in the first place and why you don't stay at home and wank

Quickly checks himself

I mean comb giraffes

Moves off left. Hand raised, miming

A voice in the class someone says We don't have any giraffes at home

Hand raised, goes on

Another voice We don't have any giraffes at home either only at the zoo but even suppose we had a giraffe at home we wouldn't be able to comb it because of the ladder we'd need a whopping great ladder to comb a giraffe

Aside

The teacher is talking on his own behind the desk

From the back behind the box

Never in my whole career

Faces audience, pulls himself together. Condescendingly

Boys you go too far when I say stay at home and comb giraffes I don't really mean to comb giraffes it's only a manner of speaking like as if I said to piss . . .

Quickly checks himself

I mean to weewee on a duck's back

Moves off right. Hand raised, mimes

A voice in the class someone says You can't weewee on a duck's back well you can but you're not allowed to on ducks they're for roasting you weewee in toilets

Hands raised, goes on

Another voice and even poohpooh if you want

Runs downstage, goes on

But Marcel says that you can poohpooh on a duck's back too but for a start it's not very easy because the feathers would tickle and they'd only swim away and secondly you're not allowed to because they're for eating

Points to the box

The teacher is getting angry

Exhausted

Leave ducks out of this we're not here to talk about ducks

Aside

There he's talking again on his own behind his desk

From the back behind the box, head in hands

Positively never in my whole career anything as much as pissing on a duck's back

Venomously, checks himself

Listen to me carefully you bunch of ignoramuses I'll give you an example let's go back to the beginning

Pause, searches

The example here it is your example you bunch of ignoramuses

Searches again, finds one

Take for example the example of the butcher

Self-importantly

But first of all does everyone know what a butcher is

Miming. The children speak hands raised. Growing satisfaction of the teacher

Everyone in unison
He's a man
Good but what else
He works in a butcher's shop
Very good but what else
He has an apprentice
Good very good and what is his apprentice called
Everyone in unison The butcher's apprentice
Well done much much better but what else
He has a wife as well
Ah ha a wife and what do you call his wife
Everyone in unison The butcher's wife
Well done excellent but what else
What else
What do you call the butcher's wife again
Everyone in unison We don't know
Except Marcel who said The Woman Butcher
Well done one gold star that's fine we can begin again

'Sits down' again behind the box, gestures sparingly

I'll go back to the beginning let's suppose boys that the butcher one morning when he got up didn't know where he was going any more why he was going when he was going so that he didn't go anymore let's suppose to kill the cows the cattle the sheep in his yard like every morning but he was mistaken that instead of killing them he starts let's suppose to stroke them with his cleaver or his pistol

Gets up, self-importantly

Well boys I'm asking you the question do

you think that you could still eat meat to grow up to be men and serve your Country if the butcher didn't go anymore in the morning into his yard that he made a mistake that he didn't know where he was going anymore or why he was going when he was going come along answer

Childlike tone

Everyone in unison says No except the voice which says Yes

Reacts strongly

Why yes

Moves off left. Childlike tone, hand raised

Because we could still eat meat

Smugly

And how could we still eat meat you stupid boy if the butcher didn't kill anyone anymore in his yard

Faintheartedly

Because if you can't eat the butcher's meat anymore you can eat the pork-butcher's meat because the pork-butcher goes every morning too into his yard to kill the pigs with his cleaver and his pistol

Aside

The teacher is talking again on his own behind his desk

Mimes

He bangs his fist on the desk

Head in his hands, then in a rage.

Positively never in my whole career mind that blockhead there

In revenge

The example is no good let's go back to the beginning

'Sits down' again behind the box

Let's suppose now boys to take a better example that the butcher not only gives up so to speak killing the cows the cattle the sheep in the morning in his yard

Lyrically

But one fair morning the pork-butcher does the same and doesn't go into his yard either anymore to kill the pigs but he too starts so to speak to stroke them

Emphatically

And let's go even further let's even suppose boys that one fair morning the same morning why not all the butchers and all the pork-butchers in the world do the same thing they all give up so to speak killing the cows the cattle the sheep the pigs anymore in their yards but stroke them forever and ever

Gets up in triumph

Well I'm asking you once again boys the question do you think boys that you could still eat meat to grow up to be men and serve your Country if all the butchers and all the pork-butchers in the world never killed anyone anymore come along answer

Pause

Everyone in unison again says No

Pause. Apprehensively

Except the voice which again says Yes

Bangs his fist on the box

Why yes

Terrorized

Because we could still

Anger

We could still what you stupid boy

Terrorized

We could still eat meat

Anger

And how could we still eat meat you stupid boy if all the butchers and all the pork-butchers in the world never killed anyone anymore

Gradually overcoming his fear

We could still eat meat because we could go and get it from all the grocers in the world because of all the grocers in the world who sell meat in tins you open them with tin openers my father has one my mother bought it for him for his birthday with a corkscrew at the other end

Aside

The teacher is crying behind his desk

Head in his hands, crying

Positively never as much as pissing on a duck's back and in my whole career

Runs downstage. Apprehensively

Marcel doesn't know what my career means either

Turning towards the box

Teacher sir what does my career mean

Runs behind the box, mimes

The teacher bangs his head against his desk

Beside himself

For pity's sake will someone tell this stupid boy immediately what my career means

Runs downstage

A voice in the classroom someone says

Hand raised

My career is like at my uncle's in Alsace his pigeons are all called careers

Polemically

But Marcel says No pigeons aren't all called careers I know careers that aren't pigeons there's paper careers and plastic careers and I've never seen them fly so you're a liar and anyway a career that can fly is called a career-pigeon.

Pointing to the box

I'm sure that teacher sir's career is not a career-pigeon

Moves to box.

Isn't that right teacher sir your career-pigeon doesn't serve our Country

Knocks the box on its side.

The teacher knocks his desk over in these circumstances I resign

Kneeling behind the box, mimes, gradually becoming aggravated

Mr Inspector would you be so kind as to herewith accept my resignation from the Pigeon Fancier's Association given the success of the racing season and the wind conditions for the career-pigeons which permit us this year to stick one up Alsace and start a carrier with your uncle and especially don't forget to take your wings Mr President I give you all my thanks and may my best wishes go with you at any rate I hope

Collapses, arms dangling over the box

Scene Six: The Stuck-Together Dogs

Drags the box downstage left. It represents the stuck-together dogs and gradually moves right. Points to the box

One day we were talking in the street what did we see on the pavement two dogs all stuck together

Behind the box, mimes

We tried to unstick them by pulling at either end

Candidly

No good dogs aren't like flies flies you can always unstick when they won't fly away not dogs and anyway dogs never fly away

Lies down behind the box

No good fancy that me and Marcel lie down on the ground to see from underneath why we couldn't unstick them

Sits up abruptly, points to the ceiling

But there's Marcel's grandmother yelling up above with her bonnet

Shouting down

Clear off from here you rascals you rogues

Aside

We didn't know whether it was at us or at the dogs

Gets up, backs away sharply

We ran for our lives

Comes back to the box, mimes.

The grandmother runs down the stairs with her broom and beats the dogs with her broom

Beating the box

Clear off from here you dirty dogs you rascals you rogues go away and do your dirty business somewhere else if my husband sees you

Aside

The grandmother is beating the dogs she's yelling the dogs are yelling too they won't come unstuck they just move up the pavement a little

Moves the box to the right, circles the stage, comes back level with the box, mimes the action

The postman arrives he sees the dogs
stuck together he tries to unstick them
with his postman's cap he beats them
with his postman's cap
It's a disgrace
The dogs are yelling they won't come
unstuck they just move up the pavement
a little

*Moves the box, circles the stage, comes
back level, mimes*

The butcher arrives with the butcher's
wife behind but he says to her
straightaway to get back behind her
counter
It's no sight for a lady
He takes some scraps from his counter
Nice doggie nice doggie
He means to unstick the dogs with his
scraps the dogs eat the scraps but they
won't come unstuck they just move up
the pavement a little

Same actions

The teacher arrives on his bicycle he
doesn't try to unstick the dogs with his
bicycle he leans his bicycle against the
wall and yells at the butcher
Go and get a sheet quickly you're
upsetting the children
Children what you see there is nothing
extraordinary you find it in books you'll
learn about it at the end of your studies
with the Senior school boys
The dogs move up the pavement

Same actions

The priest arrives in his cassock he
doesn't try to unstick the dogs he stands
between us and the dogs
The teacher says to him Well father
The priest says to him Well my son
That's nature father
That's nature my son
That's nature my children
The dogs move up the pavement

Same actions

The village policeman comes running he
doesn't try to unstick the dogs he blows
his whistle
Come on move along
The dogs don't move along the people
don't move along either he takes out his
notebook
Come on move along or I'll book you
No one wants to move along

The village policeman gets angry
First of all where are the owners

*Same actions. Doubles up, swivelling
alternately left and right*

The owners come running
Come here Rover
They try to unstick the dogs no good
They argue
Your dog always leads mine on
I'm sorry sir it's your dog that always
leads mine on
Sorry but my Rover is a well-behaved
dog you bastard
Sorry but my Rover is better behaved
than your Rover you rogue
Are you saying that my Rover is badly
behaved
That thought never crossed my mind my
dear friend I'm only saying that my
Rover is better behaved than your Rover
Better behaved than my Rover your
mongrel do you hear that Rover do you
hear that ladies and gentlemen
The owners fight but the village
policeman stands between them with his
notebook
Gentlemen that has got nothing to do
with it at the moment first of all find
some way of unsticking your dogs the law
forbids it on the public highway or I'll
book you come on let's find a vet

Same actions, gestures sparingly

The vet arrives on his vet's motorbike
with his vet's case
He gets off his bike
He goes up to the dogs
He looks at the dogs
He thinks about it
He lies down on the ground
He inspects underneath with his glasses
He feels with his hands
No problem it's not serious bring me a
bowl of water
He gets up
He picks up his glasses
He rolls up his sleeves
He speaks to the owners
Gentlemen I'm going to give you some
advice when you don't want your dog to
go out the best thing to do is to keep him
at home pass me my case

Visualizing and miming

The bowl arrives
Put it down on the ground it's us three
now chaps

Visualizing

But Marcel's father arrives too
Boys its time to go and do your
homework

Dragged by an imaginary hand

It was always time to go and do our
homework when the vet came to unstick
the dogs on the pavement we never knew
how it ended we only knew that it ended
because we saw the dogs on other days in
the street they weren't stuck together
anymore or else they were with other
dogs it wasn't always the same ones on
the pavement

Scene Seven: The Priest

*Stands still centre stage, takes the box by
the rope and drags it round the stage.
Lays it on its side, longways. Kneels
facing audience, leans on the box, playing
with it constantly.
When the child is speaking to the priest,
he looks diagonally upwards. The priest
replies directly to the audience*

At Sunday School me and Marcel would
sit down in church listening to the priest
tell us the story of the Good Lord in
heaven in paradise

Aside

I didn't know what paradise was I ask the
priest

Child's pose. Candidly

Father what's paradise

Aside

The priest thinks

Priest's pose. Unctuously

My child paradise isn't an easy thing to
explain to children

Goes on

Paradise my child is when you're old
when you've been really good you go up
to heaven with the angels everywhere
singing and flying about and the Good
Lord at the very top blessing them and
praying

Aside

I think

Child's pose

Father does he fly too

Priest's pose

No my child that's blasphemy he holds on
by himself

Same actions, gestures sparingly

I think
Father does he hang on to the ceiling
No my child that's blasphemy there is no
ceiling in heaven he holds on by himself
my child by divine grace with the baby
Jesus in his arms and his wife who's
called Mary that's why we call her the
Virgin Mary
I could understand why we call the Good
Lord's wife Mary seeing as she's called
Mary but I couldn't understand why we
called her the Virgin Mary
Father why do we call the Good Lord's
wife the Virgin Mary because if we call
her the Virgin Mary why don't we call
the butcher's wife the Virgin Mary too
she's called Mary
The priest raises his arms to heaven
That's blasphemy my child it's got
nothing to do with it
Why father has it got nothing to do with
it
Because the Good Lord's wife is in
heaven with the angels and the butcher's
wife is in the butcher's with her husband
it's got nothing to do with it
But suppose father one day the butcher's
wife goes to heaven will we call her the
Virgin Mary or just plain Mary
That's got nothing to do with it my child
for a start it's not certain that the
butcher's wife will go to heaven one day
and even suppose she does go it won't be
her who goes it will be her soul

Pause. Stunned. Same actions

Her soul I didn't know what a soul was
Father what's a soul
My child the soul isn't an easy thing to
explain to children it's something which
exists which you can't see and goes to
heaven when you're old if you've been
really good

Counts on his fingers, searches

I think Something which exists which you
can't see which goes to heaven when
you're old if you've been really good

Playful

Is it a riddle father

Lively, unctuously

No my child it's the soul

Pause, same actions

I didn't know what a soul was I didn't
even know if everyone had a soul
Father does everyone have a soul
Of course my child everyone has a soul
why would everyone not have a soul my
child
I think
Father does the butcher have a soul
The priest doesn't think
Of course my child the butcher has a soul
why would the butcher not have a soul
my child
I think
Father does the village policeman have a
soul
He doesn't think
Of course my child the village policeman
has a soul why would the village
policeman not have a soul my child

Pause. Stunned

The village policeman has a soul fancy
that

Visualizing

I could see in my head the village
policeman going up dead to heaven too
with his wings his helmet his notebook

Gets up

And I could see in my head the butcher
going up dead to heaven too with his
wings and his knives

Fantasizing

The butcher's shop going up to heaven
too with its wings behind the counter the
butcher's apprentice with his wings and
his willy everyone going up dead to
heaven with their wings

Climbs on to box, mimes

The butcher's shop was taking off the
butcher was saying his goodbyes at the
door with his knives the butcher's wife
was saying her goodbyes with one hand
counting her money behind her counter

Hallucinating

The butcher's shop takes off the butcher's
wife says to the butcher ready on your
marks flap the wings to your right Sid
and to the people watching in the street
Goodbye my friends we'll send you a

postcard

Indifferent

The people say their goodbyes in the
street with their handkerchiefs goodbye
my friends everyone says their goodbyes

Hallucinating

The butcher's shop goes up forever with
its wings it arrives in heaven you can
hardly see anything anymore just a speck
in the sky with tinted glasses

Falsely candid

The people in the street are saying Fancy
that they don't want to leave they're
looking at the sky they're looking at the
hole beside the pavement they're looking
everywhere

Brutishly

Fancy that now where are we going to
get our meat

*Gets down from the box, sits on box.
Same actions as before but the child's
questions from the opposite diagonal.
Harsher dialogue. Gestures sparingly*

Everyone has a soul I was happy I said to
myself since everyone has a soul then the
butcher's guinea-pigs have a soul too I
really liked the butcher's guinea-pigs
when me and Marcel went to stroke them
in their hutch at the butcher's
I ask the priest
Father do the butcher's guinea-pigs have
a soul
That's blasphemy my child it's got
nothing to do with it
Why father has it got nothing to do with
it
Because my child the butcher's guinea-
pigs obviously do not have a soul
Why father do the butcher's guinea-pigs
obviously not have a soul
The priest doesn't say anything more he
thinks he only says because

Pause. Hardening.

Because my child if the butcher's guinea-
pigs do not have a soul it's obvious that
the Lord in his infinite mercy didn't think
it necessary to grant them one
I didn't know what mercy meant I
pretended
Why father did the Lord not think it
necessary to grant them one in his mercy
My child if the Lord hadn't thought it

necessary to grant the guinea-pigs a soul
it's patently obvious that they aren't
worth one
Why father aren't they worth one
I am only a poor sinner I can't know
everything

Pause, gets up. Bitterly polemic

But father if the butcher's guinea-pigs
don't have a soul then no one has a soul
That has got nothing to do with it my
child guinea-pigs aren't everyone
Well who is everyone father
Everyone is only people my child and the
guinea-pigs don't belong to people
Well father who do guinea-pigs belong to
They belong to the animals my child
And who do the animals belong to father
The animals my child belong to creation
like things and people

Discouraged, sits down

I thought about it I didn't understand
anything anymore

Pause, starts again

I didn't know what creation was either
Father what's creation

Gets up. To the angels, unctuously

Creation my child is when the Lord
created everything heaven things animals
people he created everything in seven
days or rather six in the beginning it was
dark everywhere but the Lord turned on
the light to work he worked night and
day to finish everything in six days
Sunday was to rest to go to church and to
pray

Sits down again. With resentment

I thought about it I said to myself all that
in six days I think that's a bit much

Aside

I wanted to tell the priest

With animosity

Father I think that's a bit much

Aside

I wanted to tell him

Gets up angrily

Father I think the Lord was too quick he
didn't have time to give the butcher's
guinea-pigs a soul

Sits down again. Melancholy

I felt sad I really wanted to cry in the
butcher's when me and Marcel went back
to stroke the guinea-pigs

Miming

I stroked them saying to myself the Lord
was too quick when they're dead they'll
be dead forever they'll never get to
heaven they'll never get to paradise

Outraged

And I wondered if it might be better to
stay with them forever in the butcher's
rather than go up one day without them
to the heaven of the priest and the good
Lord

Holds absent look a few seconds

Scene Eight: The Corks

*Sets the box on its wheels downstage left,
at a diagonal. Sits down, propels it
diagonally backwards and stops it upstage
right. It represents the corks. Gets up.
Playful*

Me and Marcel when it rained really
loved racing corks

Visualizing, moves along diagonal

It's raining we go up the hill with our
corks we throw the corks in the water in
the gutter and they race down to the
bottom of the hill the first cork to arrive
wins

Aside

I didn't understand why it was always the
first to arrive that won mine always came
second but Marcel says

With authority

It's like the races at Brand's Hatch only
with cars it's always the first past the flag
that wins I have never seen the second
past the flag come first

Returns to the box, stops half-way

We go up the hill but one day we were
going up the hill who did we meet the
village policeman's daughter and Marcel's
sister's sister going up too they wanted to
race corks too

Magnanimously

I really like Marcel's sister's sister I lend
her a cork and Marcel lends a cork to the

village policeman's daughter

Goes to the box, moves along diagonal, visualizes

We reach the top of the hill we throw our corks we run along the gutter we cheer them on to win but not all the corks can win there are some corks which don't even budge at all they get stuck between the paving

With authority

When a cork gets stuck between the paving you're not allowed to unstick it you have to let it unstick itself on its own

Pushing the box with his foot along the diagonal

But that day Marcel cheated he had used his foot to unstick the village policeman's daughter's cork when it was stuck between the paving he thought I hadn't seen him but I had seen him

Interrupts himself, pushes once again

I cheated too I had used my foot to unstick his sister's sister's cork when it was stuck

Same action

But Marcel had seen me he had used his foot to unstick the village policeman's daughter's cork even when it wasn't stuck at all

Same action

I had seen him I unstuck his sister's sister's cork when it wasn't stuck either

Same action

Me and Marcel unstuck the corks all the way down to the bottom of the hill

Jumping with joy

His sister's sister's cork had won it was first the village policeman's daughter's cork only came second it had lost but Marcel didn't agree

With authority

The village policeman's daughter's cork came second so it's first you said so yourself

Refusing to budge

I didn't agree I said I had won when I was second because I wasn't first but that day his sister's sister's cork was first so it won

Aside

Marcel didn't agree

Obstinately

The village policeman's daughter's cork is second so it's first

With animosity

I say No I don't agree your sister's sister's cork is first so it's first

Pause. Childishly

We didn't agree we argued at the bottom of the hill I tell him Just you wait I'm going to fetch the law

Same action

But Marcel says Just you wait I'm going to fetch the police they're much stronger than the law

Miming

Me and Marcel didn't agree we fought at the bottom of the hill

Goes on, mimes

Just like at the Boxing Day ball when the butcher's apprentice fought with the pork-butcher's apprentice

Aside, candidly

They were fighting not because of the village policeman's daughter's cork but because of Marcel's sister's hairy beastie

Confidentially

The butcher's apprentice wanted to keep the hairy beastie all to himself but the pork-butcher's apprentice didn't agree he wanted to stroke the hairy beastie too

Miming

They fought they rolled on the ground they punched each other I'll smash your face in you bugger I'll knock your brains out you bastard with the people standing around cheering them on shouting Blood blood blood blood

Dazed

The butcher's and the pork-butcher's apprentices are bleeding they're bleeding

Miming

But the village policeman comes running blowing his whistle he wants them to separate Come along gentlemen you don't really want to fight now do you

Fatalistic

But the butcher's and the pork-butcher's apprentices do want to fight

Miming

The teacher comes running Come along gentlemen you don't really want to fight on Boxing Day

Fatalistic

The butcher's and the pork-butcher's apprentices separate they don't want to fight on Boxing Day

Goes upstage left

The teacher takes the butcher's apprentice by the arm and leads him into a corner and tells him off

Comes back centre. Goes upstage right

The village policeman leads the pork-butcher's apprentice into a corner and tells him off

Comes back centre. Pause

We wait a while

Motionless, visualizing

The butcher's apprentice comes out of the corner with the teacher
The pork-butcher's apprentice comes out of the corner with the village policeman

Good-natured

Come along gentlemen shake hands

Miming

The butcher's apprentice shakes the pork-butcher's apprentice's hand crying

Goes on

Come along gentlemen embrace each other

Mimes

The butcher's apprentice and the pork-butcher's apprentice embrace each other crying

Aside

The village policeman and the teacher cry too but they don't embrace each other

Goes on

Come on gentlemen let's go and have a wee drink let's go and celebrate Boxing Day

Aside

Everyone goes to celebrate Boxing Day

Pause, mimes

Everyone goes for a wee drink

Scene Nine: The Death of Marcel

Dim light. Drags the box by the rope, stops it left
Aside

One rainy day when I went to fetch Marcel to go cork racing his father says to me

Visualizing

Marcel is sick son he won't be coming to play today

Swivels to the box

I look into the room I see Marcel stretched out on his bed sleeping with white flowers everywhere and candles all around

To audience

I ask if he's going to come and play tomorrow but his father says

Visualizing

Marcel is very sick son you can only say goodbye to him you can kiss him if you like

Kneels. Kisses box noisily

I kissed Marcel I said goodbye to him

Visualizing

But I didn't understand why Marcel was sleeping with his shoes on in bed his grandmother wasn't beating him Marcel's grandmother was always beating us when we slept with our shoes on in bed

Hand raised on box

You rascals you rogues I'll teach you to sleep with your shoes on in bed

Visualizing

Marcel's grandmother wasn't beating Marcel she was praying everyone was praying

Acting surprised

But then someone arrives it's a man all in black with a black cap

Gets up, mimes. Speaks softly, suspiciously. Stiff and funeral-like

Good day ladies and gentlemen I'm sorry to disturb you we've come about the box

Confidentially

The man all in black is the boss of the men all in black there are other men all in black with black caps on the stairs the boss calls them

Pivots right, raises tone

Kindly bring in the box gentlemen and don't forget your nails Sid

To audience, lowers tone

Ladies and gentlemen every man is his own master that's why every man settles with his soul and his conscience nevertheless for young minds and for the ladies this is an altogether more delicate affair we leave the decisions at the discretion of the families represented by their head here present

Swivels right

Put the box on the floor for the moment.

To audience, visualizing

Marcel's father says to me You see these men have work to do come back tomorrow

Steps forward, clothes-conscious

I came back the next day in my Sunday best I didn't understand why I had to wear my Sunday best seeing as it was only Friday but my mother said to me It's because we're going to the funeral I knew what a funeral meant but I didn't know who was dead my mother says

Very naturally

It's Marcel who's dead son

Long pause, peers into audience

It's Marcel who's dead the caps came with the coach and the horses all in black

Goes to the box, visualizes

They take the box by the head by the feet

Spits in his hands, raises voice

That's us Sid

Visualizes

But Marcel's sister doesn't want the caps to take the box she screams she cries she fights with the caps

Confidentially

But the caps are stronger they lift up the box

Spits in his hands, grabs the box, raises his voice

That's us Sid pull a bit on your side let it go out left

Confidentially

Marcel's sister hangs on to the box but the boss tells her off

Moves off right, mimes

Come on now my dear you mustn't get yourself worked up you've got your whole life in front of you

Grabs box, drags it right

That's you Sid hold tight your end a fraction to the right good forward

Puts down box. Confidentially

Marcel's sister still wants to hang on to the box a bit longer but her father tells her off too

Moves off left, mimes

That's some way to behave do like we do do you not think these men have got something else to think about

Good-natured

Isn't that right gentlemen you've got something else to think about you'll have a wee drink

Swivels left, mimes

We will indeed we won't say no but the job comes first we'll take the box down first that'll speed us up

Pause. Visualizing

The caps take the box down the stairs one carrying each end and the boss at the bottom waving furiously saying over and over again Watch out watch out

Grabs the box, pulls it downstage, raises voice

Watch you don't knock it against the wall watch you don't knock it at the turn watch you don't miss your step wouldn't that be a fine mess speed up a bit Sid if you go on like that you'll make us late damn

Puts down box, slowly moves behind

Marcel is dead the caps slide the box into the coach with the white flowers all around

Swivels left. Funeral-like

The boss says it's time to leave all the members form a line behind the family first where is the family

Visualizing

The family all in black gets in rows behind the box

Pulls box by the rope. Slow tour of stage, comes back to starting point

The box sets off everyone follows the box
The box enters the church everyone enters the church

'Sits down' to the right of the box

Everyone sits down
The priest arrives everyone stands up but the priest says You may be seated brethren

Behind the box, miming

He raises his arms to the sky he sings he drinks from a big glass

Raises voice

You must not cry brethren

Lowers voice. Confidentially

He says that if everyone cries it's because everyone believes that Marcel is dead

Speaks louder, arms to box, then to sky

But rejoice brethren I am going to tell you the good news Marcel isn't dead he's in the life eternal

Playful

I rejoiced Marcel wasn't dead anymore the priest said so in his church

Incredulous

Marcel isn't dead anymore but the funeral goes on all the same

Pulls box by the rope. Slowly circles stage twice. Visualizing

The box is taken to the cemetery
I ask my mother out loud what does the life eternal mean but my mother says softly You mustn't speak at funerals
The box enters the cemetery
It stops at the edge of a hole

Stops box at the edge of the stage. Visualizes

Everyone stops at the edge of the hole

Pulls box up by rope, lets it fall bit by bit

The caps lower the box to the bottom of the hole

Walks around box, mimes

The priest goes up to the hole
He drops a little water on the box with his sprinkler
Everyone drops a little water
Except Marcel's grandfather who tells the priest

Doddering and trembling

Father I would really like to drop a little water too but I can't I'm a freethinker

Pause. Near the box

I came back the next day to the edge of the hole to help Marcel get out but there wasn't a hole any more just the fresh earth and the white flowers

Playful

I was happy I said to myself Marcel got out by himself I run to his father's house I go up to his bedroom but Marcel's father says to me

Looks up

Where are you going son

Climbs on to box. Looks down

I'm looking for Marcel

Gets down. Looks up

You know fine well son Marcel isn't there anymore he's dead and gone

Climbs on to box. Looks down

I say no Marcel is alive the priest said so in his church

Gets down. Upwards

They are only words my child.

Looks incredulous, runs lef.

I run to the priest

Terrified

Father Marcel's father says that Marcel is dead is Marcel dead father

Raises arms to sky

What can I say my child they are only words

Holding back tears

I cry I ask if I can soon go and see
Marcel if we can soon go cork racing

Dumbfounded, miming

The priest doesn't reply
He looks at his watch
He raises his arms to the sky

*Runs back upstage, arms fully raised
now, back to audience*

It'll soon be time for mass hurry up my
child if you want to take your first
communion one day to go one day to the
life eternal

Scene Ten: Epilogue
Unrealistic light
*Moves the box to centre, upturns it,
wheels in the air.*
*The whole scene is played as an
hallucination*

I never saw Marcel again anywhere I only
saw him in my head at night when he
told me to go and wait for him in his
bedroom

Lies down along the box

I lay down on his bed with the white
flowers and the candles all around

Sits up. Terrified

But there are the caps coming into the
room with my box

Horrified

They want to put me in the box

On his belly, holding on

I cry I hold onto the bed but the boss
tells me off

Sits down

Let's go son That's us Sid

Horrified

The caps lift me by my head by my feet

On his back, trembling

I hold on with all my strength
Everyone tells me off everyone tells me
Be a good boy

Sits down, mimes

The butcher says in the boss's ear

Lowers voice, sardonically

Why don't I take him down to the
butcher's first with my knives

Nodding his head

The grandmother makes a yes sign with
her bonnet

Action of putting on bonnet

She wants to put her bonnet on my head
he won't catch cold

*Same action. Contorted face, suggests
baby at birth*

But Marcel's sister wants to put her hairy
beastie on me that'll keep him even
warmer

Funeral-like

The boss says Let's try the gentle touch
wouldn't you like to see Marcel again son

Aside

I say yes

Jumping up

But Marcel's father says no Marcel is
dead and gone

Same action

The priest says No Marcel is in the life
eternal

Distressed

Marcel's father and the priest don't agree
they fight in the bedroom

Funeral-like

The boss says Let's go son and find
Marcel

Gets half-way into box. Sitting position

I lie down straight away in my box

Playful

Everyone applauds

Miming

Sid nails down the lid with his nails his
hammer I can't see anything anymore
just a little through the keyhole in the
box

Beaming

I'm happy I'm going to see Marcel again

Funeral-like, miming

The boss says it's time for all the
members to fall in line ladies and
gentlemen the family first where is the

family

Visualizing

There isn't any family but there's six dogs
stuck together coming all stuck together
We're the family

Miming

The boss tries to unstick them with his
black cap

Faintheartedly

The dogs aren't happy You're not
allowed to separate the family

Animal-like

The butcher says In that case I'll run and
get my scraps

Miming

He comes back with his guinea-pigs and
his knives I don't have any more scraps
no matter I'll make some in the church

Visualizing

All the members fall in line
The butcher's wife joins the members
with her counter
The butcher's apprentice joins the
members with his willy three sizes
bigger than the Senior school boys who
join the members from the rear
with the janitor of the sweets and
cigarettes
The village policeman joins the members
with his notebook and his pencil
The teacher with his bike and his ducks
All the members fall in line

Goes on

The butcher's apprentice says to the
pork-butcher's apprentice to fall in with
the members at the front and to Marcel's
sister to fall in with the pork-butcher's
apprentice's members who says to him
No you were here before me but the
butcher's apprentice says It doesn't
matter I'll fall in from the rear the
funeral can begin

Spins the wheels frenetically

The coach sets off with the members
following and they enter the church

Mimes

The priest raises his arms to the sky

Raises his voice

Let there be no mistake brethren I have

a willy too

Mimes

He lifts up his cassock
He shows the members his willy
He dips his willy in the holy water
He shakes the water over the members
with his willy

Ecumenically

Rejoice brethren

Visualizes and mimes

The members rejoice in the church
The pork-butcher's apprentice rejoices
with the butcher's apprentice stroking the
hairy beastie of Marcel's sister who
rejoices by stroking the butcher's and the
pork-butcher's apprentices' willies with
her hands
The janitor rejoices by stroking with her
tongue the willies of the Senior school
boys who give her smoking cigarettes
The village policeman rejoices with his
notebook and his pencil
The butcher with his guinea-pigs and his
knives
The butcher's wife with her money
behind the counter
The grandmother with her bonnet and
her broom
The teacher with his bike and his ducks
The priest with his willy and his sprinkler

Goes on

Every single member rejoices

Narcissistically

I rejoice too all alone in my box because
I'm going to see Marcel again soon

Spins wheels frenetically

The coach sets off

Hallucinating more and more

It arrives at the cemetery with the
members following they enter the
cemetery they stop at the edge of the
hole

*Starting from the wings a single
spotlight isolates the box.
Slowly lies down*

The caps lower my box to the bottom of
the hole

Distressed

But Marcel isn't at the bottom of the
hole

Points to ceiling

I'm all alone at the bottom of the hole with every single member above leaning over and looking down at the bottom of the hole

Tries to sit up, hand stretched out

I want out I want to go home I ask the members to help me

Fails, lies down

But the members are laughing at the edge of the hole Come on let's go and rejoice somewhere else brethren

Tries to sit up

I ask my mother

Fails, lies down

But my mother says Be a good boy son you're not allowed to speak when you're dead

Tries once again

I ask the priest

Sits up laboriously, speaks down.

I speak louder Father my mother says I'm dead I'd like to know if I'm dead father

Pause. Distressed

The priest doesn't answer he only shakes a little water on my box with his willy

Raises voice

I speak louder Father I'd like to know if I'm in the life eternal

Pause. Distressed

The priest shakes a little water What can I say my child they are only words

Raises voice

I speak louder I ask if I'll get out of the hole one day if I'll go home one day

Pause. Distressed

What can I say my child they are only words
With a little water

Shouting. More and more distressed

I speak louder I shout from the bottom of the hole I ask why Marcel isn't at the bottom of the hole if Marcel is at the bottom of another hole if we'll soon be able to go cork racing

Pause. Terrorized

The priest doesn't answer he shakes a little more water with his willy then he goes away for good with the members laughing

Protects his face with his arms

I can't see anyone anymore I can't see anything anymore because Sid is throwing soil on top of my box

Pause

I can only hear the members in the distance withdrawing and laughing

Further and further away

What can I say my child they are only words my child they are only words my child they are only words my child they are only words

*Fairly long pause.
Arms at sides, eyes closed.
Slowly, carefully*

They are only words

BLACKOUT.

*For little Sophie.
Chartainvilliers, August 1984*

STRANGER IN THE HOUSE

Translated by Helen Garner

RICHARD DEMARCY has written more than fifteen plays, many of which have been performed by the 'Naïf Théâtre' run by him and his wife, Teresa Motta. His plays deal with modern myths and fables presented in a comic style that embraces elements of both the grotesque and the matter-of-fact. Demarcy's most recent work includes an operatic version of an earlier play *La Grotte d'Ali (Ali's Cave)* (1986) and *Les Rêves de Lolita et Laverdure (Lolita's Dreams and Laverdure)* (1987). He is the author of a study of the role of live entertainment in contemporary society: *Éléments d'une sociologie du spectacle*, 1973. A satire of contemporary racial attitudes *Stranger in the House* was written for half a dozen actors and includes music, mime and comedy routines borrowed from traditional cabaret.

L'Étranger dans la Maison was first presented at the Théâtre de la Tempête, Cartoucherie de Vincennes, Paris, on 15 January 1982.
The play was performed by Alain Aithnard, Saïd Amadis, Gilette Barbier, Jean-Claude Broy, Etienne Marest, Teresa Motta, Jean Obé and Bernard Spiegel.

Directed and designed by Richard Demarcy
Lighting by Pierre Rovai
Music and songs by Saïd Amadis.

Helen Garner's translation was first read at the Riverside Studios, London, in January 1986.

Characters

The MOTHER
The FATHER
The CHILDREN   Marcel
                               Little Julie
                               Little Louis
                               Little Germain
The STRANGER   Zerbi Larbi of Barbary on the shores of Araby
The KING
The COOK   Gorillo alias Mademoiselle Marguerite
The MOUNTED POLICEMAN
The ONE-MAN BAND

A rectangle of red carpet surrounded at the sides by gravel and in front by a ditch full of dead leaves.
   A door upright in its frame in the middle of the space divides the inside of the house from the outside.
   Outside: snow falling from the ceiling, a freezing wind, frost, gravel, dead leaves.
   Inside: red floor, an imposing wardrobe at the back, two big beds like islands: one, for the children, with red and white sheets, the other for the parents with red, white and blue sheets.
   A little round table with a loaf of bread and a knife stuck in it, the axe and the chopping block near the door, brooms for various purposes . . . Perhaps, between the red floor and the dead leaves, three signboards hanging on a wire, reading ELECTRIC FENCE, SAVAGE DOG, BOOBY-TRAPPED HOUSE.

Prologue

The parents are asleep in their bed. The children are busily playing their favourite game (e.g. with the house broom, the game of 'broken-down motorbike' or 'bed-boat-raft-canoe'). The stranger, dressed in a black coat, is sweeping with his long streetsweeper's broom the dead leaves that separate the house from the front row of the audience. He gathers up a pile of leaves and, tired, falls asleep in it. His sleep is troubled. The children approach him, stopping in the middle of their 'bed-boat-raft' voyage.

LITTLE JULIE. Hey! Mister! Mister!
   Are you dreaming, mister?
   Are you dreaming or sleeping?

STRANGER (*emerging from the pile of leaves*) Ah! yes, I was dreaming. I was dreaming of a story from long, long ago.
   The plot is so strong that I still dream about it.

LITTLE GERMAIN (*astonished*). Do you really mean to say
   The past will never go away?
   No sooner do we dream and snore
   Than it comes creeping back once more?

LITTLE LOUIS (*very sure of himself*).
   Of course it can!
   The past is as strong as the potato blight
   That kills the potatoes in the night.

STRANGER. As you say, my golden-headed boy, 'as strong as the potato blight that kills the potatoes in the night'. If you like, children, I'll tell you a story.

The children look at each other as if to make sure they all agree, then LITTLE JULIE *decides.*

JULIE. If it's a tale
   that'll make us wail
   if it's a story
   all bloody and gory
   then Little Germain
   and Little Louis
   and Little Julie
   will all agree.

Lights down. The cold wind rises.

STRANGER. Once upon a time in the depths of winter there was a terrible frost outside, and inside the house was pierced by dreadful draughts . . .

Blackout. The wind has risen in fury around the sleeping house. The stranger has disappeared, and so have the signboards.

Departure

Sleep and silence in the bedroom. In their bed the children are gently snoring: three pretty little snouts poke out over the collective sheet. Further over, the father and the mother are all tangled up in their blue, white and red sheets. Beside the bed, a pile of Police Detective *and other magazines with resounding titles, obviously the father's favourite reading matter . . . The father and mother, as usual, have been wrangling over the blanket and have ended up dividing it between them: toes can be seen sticking out but they seem to be asleep.*

FATHER (*lighting the bedside lamp*). Psst! The children are sleeping like little logs! Come on!

They get up and stealthily drag out the corpse of the eldest child, which they hide in the cupboard.

MOTHER (*towing the corpse by its feet: it's already stiff as a board*). You needn't have fired at Ernest. You could at least have shot Little Louis. Little Louis is the greatest cross I have to bear, the unwanted child that refused to be aborted.

FATHER. I fired at something that was moving in the bloody hall! How was I to know it was only Ernest creeping out to the kitchen to get a drink of water? It was just a shot of bad luck, that's all.

They hide the body in the cupboard.

MOTHER. If you don't look out, Marcel, we'll be losing our family allowance! For heaven's sake be more careful next time. (*Passing the children's bed she casts the tender gaze of the clucky mother.*) Now all we've got left is these three tender little blossoms.

They go back to bed.

FATHER. Don't worry. I'll give you another one, you can even get a baby bonus. (*Pulling off his braces, a slipper, a sock, etc.*) Might as well get down to business right away. Right now! Come on, let's get cracking.

He slides into the bed. A lot of vigorous bouncing goes on under the red, white and blue sheet, a real flag floating in the wind.

MOTHER. Get away, Marcel, you horrible great brute! You've no respect for Ernest's soul on its way up to heaven with its lovely pink cheeks and its little angel's wings . . . (*She gives him a couple of good whacks with the bolster, then turns her back on him, taking all the blanket.*) You're like a train coming into the station!

She imitates the sound of a train puffing into the station, then fades into snoozing, sign of deep and restful sleep. Marcel, after wandering with his sheet round the space, comes back to bed.

CHILDREN. Psst! Psst! They're asleep. Come on!

They get out of the blankets and get the grandfather's body out from under the bed.

JULIE. You certainly did a good job on Grandpa.

LOUIS. Daddy always said, 'Don't hesitate, Little Louis! If it moves, shoot! Shoot anything that moves in the night. Don't hesitate.' I didn't even have time to aim. 'Who goes there? Show your papers! State your name and business!' I went through all the formalities, just like on TV, so as not to cause a regrettable incident – and crash, bang, thump, down goes Grandpa like a sack of potatoes. No hope of bringing him back to life, no matter how hard I twisted his nose and his big toe.

GERMAIN. He must have got such an awful fright
That his poor old heart, which was none too bright
And worn out with labour, gave up the fight
And he went out like a light.

JULIE. That's what comes of climbing walls at his age.

They hide the corpse, stiff as a plank, in the cupboard.

JULIE. Now what are we going to do? What if they find him?

GERMAIN (*coming out of the cupboard shaking his blood-stained hands*). Hang on a minute! Don't lock it. There's blood all over the floor of the cupboard. I'll wipe my hands on my trouser pockets.

MOTHER *stirs in her sleep.*

JULIE. Shhh! They're waking up. Quick – back to bed!

Silence. Utter calm. We hear the icy wind blowing outside. The MOTHER *turns on the bedside lamp.*

MOTHER. My orbs are struck with such visions! I can't sleep. Marcel, wake up! I'm full of forebodings. Marcel! I'm sure it's our Ernest up there in heaven. He's not at all happy about the way he was treated – about the peremptory and authoritarian manner in which you packed him off to sleep in his hole in the cemetery. (*Spotting several empty cartridges scattered on the end of the bed.*) And now how do you expect to practise self-defence? Eh? You haven't even got any ammunition left. Eh? (*Looks him scornfully up and down, him and his hunting gun.*) As a soldier, my dear, you don't really cut the mustard! (*Hallucinations overwhelm her again.*) Oh! before these glassy orbs of mine such visions dance and twine!

FATHER (*face in pillow*). Go back to sleep. I've set the traps out there
To tear the flesh of robber, wolf or bear
That tiptoes from the forest, eyes aglare.

At that moment, someone knocks at the door. Wind in the trees. Snow falling.

MOTHER. Marcel, Marcel, wake up!
There's someone at the door!
The cold is shocking,
And there's someone knocking.
Who can it be, in this snow so deep,
Waking a family from righteous sleep?

STRANGER (*outside the door, in the snow*). Open the door! Open the door!

FATHER (*to the tousled children, who wake with a jump, chilly-nosed, eyes*

peering over the sheet. The littlest one runs to peep through the keyhole).
Don't open it! Don't touch the door!
Not till he tells us what he's looking for.
Whether you're friend or whether you're foe,
Be on your way in the ice and snow!
And if it's the Red Cross collector,
we've already made a donation – more than one! (*He hides under the covers. To the children.*) Nobody move!

Outside, galloping hooves can be heard, coming closer.

STRANGER (*knocking again*). Open the door! Open the door!

Silence. The FATHER signals to his offspring to keep quiet. The MOTHER, dishevelled, sits up in bed. Suspense. Squeakings of the door. The door opens very slowly.

MOTHER. Marcel! Someone's coming in! Someone's trampling into our intimate private life! (*Sees the door open wider.*) And who on earth left that door unlocked again?

FATHER. It must have been Ernest, before he went to bed. I did the right thing when I wiped him out.

GERMAIN. It must be Grandpa, coming back from one of his mad escapades.

The door opens a bit more and a hand throws a big broom through the crack. They all step back, terror-stricken. ZERBI LARBI pushes the door and it opens wide.

CHILDREN (*sitting up in bed*). Axe! Drama! Crime!
Noose and cat-o'-nine!
Bash, bite, drown in lime!
Axe! Drama! Crime!

MOTHER. Oh, God, it's the stranger.
He's forced his way in.
Bad as the devil
And blackened with sin.

GERMAIN. Maybe it's only Santa Claus
With presents for all the girls and boys?

FATHER. More likely a bandit, escaped from jail
With police dogs hot on his trail.

The stranger has stayed at the door. At these last words of the FATHER's he slams the door shut behind him. A storm bursts in the sky and the lightning flashes quite close: the fuses blow. Cries of fear in the dark. The light comes back on. ZERBI is alone in the space examining the FATHER's gun which he's bumped into. Softly the CHILDREN, the MOTHER and the FATHER come out of the cupboard and from under the bed.*

MOTHER. Who are you? What do you want?
Where are you from and where do you think you are going to?

ZERBI. My name is Zerbi
Zerbi Larbi of Barbary on the shores of Araby.
The police are on my tail!
There's Dangerous Dan the punter, Detective Sprat
And Jack the Hat
And Scarface Lionel the well-known migrant hunter.

Wind and galloping without.

ZERBI. And if anybody so much as coughs . . .

LOUIS (*very knowledgeably, to his little sister*). Because if you cough, Mister Araby will
Cut you up in little slivers,
Mince you up like chicken livers,
Then he'll make you into a big salami
And flog you off to the army.
Isn't that what you taught us, Dad, about why Arabs are so bad?

JULIE. Oh! Mister Zerbi
Please have mercy (y)
We wouldn't make a good salami (i)
Even for the army (y).

GERMAIN. Oh yes, oh please, oh Mister Zerbi!
Let us live – oh, please have mercy!
After all
We're very, very small!

LOUIS. (Ooh)

MOTHER. Now he's forced his way inside
And locked the door behind him tight
He'll cut our throats and bleed us white
And leave us lying in the freezing night!

ZERBI *goes up to the cupboard, sniffing.*

CHILDREN. Axe! Drama! Crime!
Torture! Guillotine!
Crash! Bash! Mash! Slime!
Axe! Drama! Crime!

The sound of a galloping horse in the distance, coming closer. Sepulchral silence. Everyone stops. Elastic ears stretch on alert heads.

MOTHER. Marcel, I hear a noise.
They're heading this way, at a gallop.

FATHER. They're after the Zerbi!
(*Sitting up in bed.*)
It's the police! Hurray! Hurray!
The gallant lads are on their way.
It's Mister Plod and Mick the Mod
And Constable Grab and Sergeant Stab
And Inspector Chevrolet.
Alarm! Alarm!

ZERBI *picks up the knife that was stuck in the table and hurls himself on* MARCEL *to make him shut up. Shining blade against white throat – image dreamed of by millions of native French citizens who absolutely adore being afraid of the foreigners in their midst; as* LITTLE LOUIS *has already said above, and as can be verified any Saturday in the métro.*

ZERBI. When I was a little boy
A shepherd in Barbary of Araby
With my cousins Abdallah and Kadaif of Mascara
So my mother Fatma could make the couscous
I was the one who used to slit the ewe's throat.
I can handle a knife like lightning.
I know how to do the whole flock.
Even the
Lambs. So – not a sound. Get it?

CHILDREN. Yes, Mister Zerbi Larbi – we get it!

ZERBI. And in the terrible war of Barbary
The sentry in the night . . .
So – get it? – not a peep out of you!

Outside, the policeman, making a couple of turns on his horse, has stopped in front of the door. He empties the water out of his boots and looks through the keyhole. LITTLE GERMAIN *runs to look and as usual*

pokes an old sword through the keyhole. Luckily for his eye the policeman stands up just in time. A froggy chorus sounds from the swamp. Snow falls from the ceiling.

MOUNTED POLICEMAN (*knocking at the door*). Police! Mounted police,
From the gang of Commissioner Grim
You've heard of him
And Detective Sprat
And Inspector Rat
It's the law enforcement agents
Is anyone home?

MOTHER (*after a hesitation*). Our whole family's here, and we're all sound asleep.

POLICE. What about your husband?

MOTHER. He's here as well, but he's very busy. He mustn't be disturbed.

POLICE. You wouldn't happen to have seen an Arab?
A tall one with a moustache
And a long, very sharp and very pointy knife?

MOTHER. There are Arabs everywhere,
But we don't have any around here.

POLICE. His two front teeth are solid gold
His bottom ones of silver cold
And when he walks he's pigeon-toed.

MOTHER. We haven't seen any Arab answering to that description.

POLICE. Make sure your locks are tight.
You could get a nasty fright
If he came knocking in the middle of the night.
As well he might.

POLICEMAN *gets back on his horse, makes a couple of turns and gallops off again into the cold night. The kids nick across to the keyhole and a distant owl takes up the frogs' chorus.* ZERBI *lets* MARCEL *go and, checking around, approaches the cupboard, sniffing. He mumbles in Arabic, mixing the two languages.*

ZERBI. There's a very funny smell coming out of this cupboard.

The kids, who were keeping watch at the door, rush to put themselves between him and the forbidden cupboard.

CHILDREN. Axe! Drama! Crime!
Cram and Stuff and Shrink and Slime!
Dog and Rat and Snake and Swine!
Axe! Drama! Crime!

MOTHER (*also stepping in his path with soup tureen and bowls*). Mister Zerbi Larbi, now you've made yourself at home, won't you stay for supper?

GERMAIN. Oh yes! Please do, Mister Zerbi Larbi. Stay with us and share our dinner. It's a nice soup, made of turnips and parsnips and swedes.

ZERBI. Thank you, little blondie. (*Also glancing cautiously into the tureen in which float three shrivelled turnips.*) But keep this nice vegetable soup for yourselves. All I need is money, supplies and new clothes. I'll just wait till this storm and the rotten wind blow over, and then I'll be on my way, before there's more trouble.

FATHER. How am I supposed to have an appetite?
With him around I couldn't take a single bite.
The soup would taste like mud
With him just waiting to spill my blood.

MARCEL, *who for some time has been fumbling under the bed, perhaps in search of a full cartridge, fits deed to thought and grabs the knife stuck in the loaf of bread on the table, walks across the bed and advances on ZERBI who has his back turned. The MOTHER sees him and drops the soup tureen.*

MOTHER. Marcel!

CHILDREN (*also dropping their plates*). Marcel!

ZERBI, *quick as lightning, spots the danger and seizes the axe which was near the door, stuck in the log. MARCEL already has the bolster in his hand, ready for close combat. The CHILDREN give rhythm to this skirmish with their fierce counting rhyme 'Axe, Drama, Crime' – while the MOUNTED POLICEMAN comes back, prancing on his horse in front of the door. Fight: Bolster and knife against old axe. Feathers fly.*

ZERBI (*hearing the policeman and brandishing the axe*). Shut up! Or I'll –

LOUIS (*pleased to show he knows how stories go*). Yes, shut up, Marcel, or else
Mister Arab will cut you up in little slivers, mince you up like chicken livers,
and then he'll make you into a big salami
and flog you off to the army.
That's right, isn't it, Mister Zerbi?

ZERBI. That's it exactly, boy. You've got a good memory for what your daddy taught you.

JULIE. Me too, Mister Zerbi, I've understood it too!

GERMAIN. Little Germain understands too! We read it in the papers, and heard it on the news. The telly's broken down, so that's no good any more but in the shops we hear plenty of people talking, And we've understood everything our daddy's taught us 'cause our daddy's smart.

The POLICEMAN has stopped outside the door, emptied water out of his boots again and looked through the keyhole. He gets back on his horse and rides off. MARCEL throws the pillow at ZERBI who, with a couple of flourishes of the axe and brandishings of the tomahawk, drives his adversary back.

ZERBI. Come on, hurry up! Put that cutlass down! They don't muck around, you know, Inspector Rat's gang and Scarface the migrant hunter.

(MARCEL *has backed as far as the table and stuck his knife into it. He comes back with his head down, dragging his feet. While* MOTHER *and* CHILDREN *pick up the pieces of the tureen with dustpan and brush,* ZERBI *sits fanning himself at the table.*)
I've got no choice now. I've been turned into an outlaw. I need money for a train, the métro, a taxi from here to Paris. I need a disguise.

MOTHER (*bucket and broom in hand*). If we die we won't be able to tell you what we've got.

ZERBI (*noticing the sheep-like manner in which she says this*). And what have you got, apart from this fridge, this TV, this bed cover, this washing-machine and those sheepish eyes?

ZERBI *goes towards the cupboard as he says these words. The* CHILDREN *block his path again, to defend the 'sanctuary'.*

CHILDREN. Nothing! Nothing! Not a thing!
Not even a piece of string!
Or a piece of rope
Or a bar of soap
No cigs, no wigs,
Not a thing to wear
Not even a comb to comb our hair
The cupboard's bare
We swear

GERMAIN *and* JULIE. It's not that we want to hurt your feelings,
But there's no potatoes, only peelings.
Our shoes have no soles,
Our trousers are all full of holes.
No rugs, no blankets for our beds.
The key is stuck, the lock is dead.
There's nothing here worth stealing.

JULIE. Even our saucepans have no lids.
We know it's impolite
To offer not a single bite
But our parents had too many kids
And the family's on the skids.

MARCEL (*stops pacing*). The kids are right. Our life's so humble
That I might have dropped my bundle
And fallen into despair
If I didn't know that in the shed out there
In the wood that groans with cold
There's a safe left over from the war
And it's full of silver and gold.

ZERBI. A safe? A safe, round here?

MARCEL. Yes! A safe, a great big safe.

ZERBI. I would appreciate being told
The precise whereabouts of this safe of gold.

MARCEL. It's in the shed, like I said.
Over yonder, past the pond.

ZERBI. Tell your kids to get out of bed
And bring the safe in from the shed.

MARCEL. My children? They're too weak and thin.
It'd take two strong men to drag it in.

ZERBI. How do you know what's in the safe, anyway?

MARCEL (*embarrassed*). Well . . . it's a bit hard to explain.

MOTHER. Drop it, Marcel. I'll tell Mister Zerbi of Araby everything. If you do it, you'll end up annoying us by getting it all mixed up and telling it in bits. (*She tells. The one-man band creates the fantastic background to the story – crickets, frogs, waterfowl, suspense.*) 'Twas on a lovely summer's day
Our little family set out to play
And picnic merrily beneath a tree.
Old Sol sent down his golden beam
Upon the charming rustic scene
And I began to serve our simple tea.
But hark! Marcel! What is this sound I hear
That falls so harsh upon the ear?
Why, only the rustle of a passing dog
Who, leaping over swamp and log
Goes hunting waterbird and frog . . .
No sooner do I open up our basket
Than a man comes hobbling by
Dragging his right leg and an extremely heavy casket.

CHILDREN. The famous safe, Mummy?

MOTHER. Indeed it was, my dears, the famous safe!
Quick as a flash we hid behind a tree,
Marcel, the kids and me,
And there we held our breath
In a silence deep as death.
And do you know what it was?

CHILDREN. What was it, Mummy?

MOTHER. A soldier with a wounded foot,
Dirty and tired, with only one boot,
And dragging behind him as he went
The safe belonging to his regiment.

CHILDREN. And then what happened, Mummy?

MOTHER. Then all of a sudden, in they come!
The other army, with fife and drum!
We all crouched down behind our tree.

GERMAIN (*the smallest, crouching down small*). We crouched down tiny, didn't we Mum?
About as tiny as a crumb?

MOTHER. Indeed we did, my darling,
Smaller than the smallest crumb,
Smaller than Tom Thumb.

JULIE. And then what happened, Mum?

MOTHER. Because of the trail of blood

behind him,
It didn't take them long to find him.
He didn't have a chance.

ZERBI. And did they find the safe?

MARCEL (*who's been pacing up and
down but now stops*). No! Lucky for
us, the man preferred
To die like a hero, without a word.
He kept the secret under his lid,
And I'm the only one who knows
where the safe is hid.

ZERBI. So far so good.
But why did you leave it out in the
wood?
Specially in this kind of
neighbourhood.
Why don't you bring it home and hide
it, –
Lock this cupboard with the safe inside
it?

WOMAN. Ah! Mister Zerbi Larbi of
Araby! (*half swooning*) You've no idea
How hard life is in this country!
So desperate is your modern thief
He wouldn't scruple to steal your very
handkerchief.

FAMILY (*in turns, MOTHER,
FATHER, CHILDREN, percussion by
the one-man band and the
CHILDREN*). Nothing can keep them
out!
People like that don't bother to knock.
They come at any tick of the clock,
Their pockets with screwdrivers
chockablock,
And even the famous Lockwood triple
lock
To them is a laughing-stock.
Nothing is sacred!
They are violators.
They rip open the door of the
refrigerator.
And smear molasses
And even our grandmother's special
glasses,
Our precious Venetian family crystal
Is put to the sword
With jackboot and pistol.
The soup goes down
With a guzzle and slurp
The cutlets and chops
They bolt in one gulp.
Then on to the dining-room, where
these jackanapes
See fit to attack the Regency drapes

And tear them up to make Batman
capes.
They trample on the china jugs
And rip out phone wires
And electric plugs
And swing from the chandelier
Like a pack of jungle apes.
In the bedroom
With their grubby paws
They rape
And rifle
The chest-of-drawers,
Slit open bedding
For jewellery
And cash
And bounce
And jounce
Upon the mattresses
Until the bedsteads smash.
And what goes on *between* the sheets,
No doubt,
Are things that kids are not allowed to
think about.
Out in the yard
They take our trikes
And scooters
And ride them and crash them
And hoot the hooters.
Then sozzled
And laughing
And hiccuping
And in disarray
They rev up their big black motorbikes
And they ride away

*As she says these last words, the
MOTHER in her turn seizes the knife.
She too has been overcome by an access
of murderous folly.*

CHILDREN. Mummy!

ZERBI. Right! (*A phrase or two in
Arabic.*)
I'm going to start counting
And by the time I get to ten
I want to see your wife tied up
Like a big fat roasting hen.
And as for you, you great big ox,
You can go out and find the famous
money-box.
You don't look tough
But you're strong enough.
It'll do you good to pull up your socks.
I'll stay here with the children and your
wife
And keep sharpening the blade of this
shining knife.
One!

The one-man band punctuates the count. MARCEL *ties up the* MOTHER *with the hose which is fixed on to the tap: a very tricky job. This could be a kind of Arabic lesson:* ZERBI *counts in Arabic and little by little the kids repeat the numbers. Inversion of the colonial lesson.*

CHILDREN. Axe!

ZERBI. Two!

CHILDREN. Drama!

ZERBI. Three!

CHILDREN. Crime!

ZERBI. Four.

CHILDREN. Red in tooth and claw.

ZERBI. Five.

CHILDREN. Still alive.

ZERBI. Six.

CHILDREN. Thundersticks.

ZERBI. Seven.

CHILDREN. Go to heaven.

ZERBI. Eight.

CHILDREN. Shut the gate.

ZERBI. Nine.

CHILDREN. Hang your britches on the line.

JULIE. Nine, nine and a half, nine and three-quarters, ten!

The CHILDREN *make the noise that goes with the gesture of drawing a knife across the throat. At that moment the* FATHER *ties the last knot.*

FATHER. There you are. She's all tied up like a half-cooked sausage. Farewell.

CHILDREN (*The Farewell Song*).
Farewell, Daddy, farewell, Mummy,
Heart-rending farewell.
The village bell tolls out its knell
We wish him well, goodbye Marcel –
Painful farewell.
Farewell, Daddy, farewell, Mummy.

FATHER. Farewell, wife
Farewell, children
Germain, Julie and Louis.

MOTHER. Husband, farewell.
My darling Marcel,

Going out to brave the icy lake
For your family's sake.
Beware of forest rangers,
And don't talk to strangers,
And return bedeck'd in gold and glory
To tell your story.

FATHER. You stay here and keep the home fires burning.
Before you know it, I'll be returning.

He goes out. From outside the door, in the wind and frost.

Phew! So much for the bloody family.
If they think the swamp's my destination
They're in for a nasty revelation.
Do they really think I'd bother?
Forget it! I'm going home to Mother.
The whole damn crew is driving me crazy.
The boys are stupid, the girl is lazy.
The youngest's always got his fingers up his nose
And Julie picks her toes.
The mother can talk the leg off an iron pot,
And who's to say they're even mine, the kids she's got?
When a fellow's stuck with parasites like these,
The only thing to do is fan the breeze.
Bravo, Marcel!
I think you'll manage very well.

He sings one last couplet before vanishing into the night.

Farewell, children,
Farewell, wife.
I may return richer than I was when I went,
Dragging the cashbox of the regiment.
But then again perhaps I won't
So if you'd thought of waiting – don't.
Meanwhile – heart-rending farewells.

The CHILDREN *have stayed on the doorstep waving their hankies as the* FATHER *plunges off into the snow falling in the night. As soon as he has disappeared, the little girl 'attacks' – asking the burning, hasty questions of kids who wriggle like worms with pleasure and curiosity.*

JULIE. Phew! At last he's gone, the rotten old windbag, with his hopelessly out-of-date ideas.

GERMAIN. Good riddance to bad

rubbish!
I hope he slips and breaks a bone
And never comes back home.
Phew!
And now without his aggravation
We can have a proper conversation.

JULIE. Mister Zerbi Larbi,
Is it really true what we've been told
That Barbary is the richest country in
the world,
That silken flags are there unfurled,
That the streets are paved with mother-
of-pearl?

ZERBI. Indeed it's true, my blondie girl.

JULIE. And, Mister Larbi,
Is it true what we've been told,
In Barbary wherever you dig a hole
Big squirts of oil worth more than gold
Come shooting out all uncontrolled?

ZERBI. Indeed it's true, my one-toothed
child.

LOUIS. Mister Zerbi Larbi, is that why
in our country we see all the brothers
and cousins from your country always
digging holes in the street?

ZERBI. That's why, my little louse-
headed boy.

GERMAIN. Here people are always
talking at the dinner table about
Barbary of Araby, and Mister Zerbi
Larbis like you, and about the oil
crisis, and everybody's wondering
whether we're going to eat energy.

LOUIS (correcting). If we're going to run
out of energy.

ZERBI. People shouldn't talk with their
mouth full.

JULIE. Mister Zerbi Larbi, is it true that
you're going to buy up all of France
and make it a part of Barbary?

ZERBI. It's true, little blondie.

GERMAIN. And England too?

ZERBI. Yes.

LOUIS. And America too?

ZERBI. Yes.

JULIE. And Russia too?

ZERBI. Yes.

A silence. The CHILDREN look at
each other, wondering about a lot of
things.

GERMAIN. And is it true that you won
against the French in the great war of
Barbary?

ZERBI. It's true.

LOUIS. So they're pretty hot stuff then,
the people of Barbary?

ZERBI. Very hot stuff, my little nit-
head.

GERMAIN. And is it true that the other
side had cannons and planes and boats,
and the Zerbis only had little knives?

ZERBI. Yes, it's true.

LOUIS. And is it true that in Barbary
people drive right across the desert in
great big huge cars?

ZERBI. It's true.

GERMAIN. And is it even true that
dromedaries and camels have round
humps on their backs because of
having to walk on all fours over the
wavy dunes in the desert?

ZERBI. It's true, my little toothless
wonder.

JULIE (sighing pleasurably. Behind, the
MOTHER gives a little cough and
wriggles, still tied up in the hose). What
a beautiful country!
Oh, Zerbi Larbi, do be nice –
Undo our mother in a trice
Before the hose begins to slice
Her twice or thrice.

ZERBI sets the MOTHER free.

GERMAIN (producing a sheet of paper
he's found in his schoolbag). And later,
will you draw me a barbie? Promise?

ZERBI. I promise, little blondie.

JULIE. Now, Mister Zerbi Larbi,
Slowly, truthfully, carefully,
Weightily, and with melancholy,
Will you tell us your life story?

GERMAIN. And while you're talking,
Mummy and me will tidy the house up,
lovingly.

Here will be a long song, sung by
ZERBI about his brushes with the
police.

ZERBI (The song of Zerbi the Street-
Sweeper).
In the streets of Paris

From Belleville to the Champs-Élysées
I push my broom, I sweep the dirt
away.
I am the sweeper, all the livelong day.

People bring their poodles out to poo
Their names are Fifi, Foufou and
Loulou.
The animals are spoilt rotten,
Or they've been taught and have
forgotten,
Anyway they are not good.
They never do their business where
they should.
Under my breath a curse I mutter
As I sweep the poodle shit into the
gutter.

Into the mighty Paris railway stations
Gare du Nord, Gare de l'Est,
Come the trains full of travellers.
One day, if I ever get away,
To be a shepherd in the wilds of
Barbary,
I'll christen all my ewes
The names the Frenchmen choose –
Foufou, Loulou, Fifi,
To remind me of the doggies of Paris.

The girls go past, the famous Paris girls
Their hair is plaited or it hangs in curls
Even the ones on bicycles so free
They all look like poodles to Zerbi
Larbi.
Back home, on the other side,
I have cousins who live far and wide –
Kamel Abdullaia Fortich
And Zerma de Mascara
But I was born in rue de Monzaia
Right near the rue de Pelleport
Between the barracks and the fort.
I'm practically a Frenchman born and
bred
Though they'd be really shocked to
hear it said.

The CHILDREN *applaud.*

JULIE. You sing so well, Zerbi!
One day on the footpath at Denfert-
Rochereau
Two blokes pull out knives and are
having a go
One gets it in the guts and sinks down
slow.

GERMAIN *and* ZERBI. I am the
swarthy one, so the coppers seize
My little pocket knife that hardly cuts
through cheese.
But the stabbed one was a good bloke.

He saw the cops grab me and up he
spoke:
'Let him go,' he says, 'it wasn't the
wog.
He was sweeping the gutter, just doing
his job.'
'Give us the broom,' says the
interrogator.
They hit first and ask questions later.
Thank you, gentlemen, for your grace
and favour.

ZERBI (*takes up the song solo. Spoken/
sung*). Then I worked on a market stall
'Cabbages! Lettuces!' I used to call
But the boss didn't like my accent at
all.

MOTHER (*from the distance sings too.
They all turn admiringly toward her;
she has a beautiful operatic voice*). One
unhappy day the cucumbers disappear
Someone has laid hands on them, I
fear
Oh foolish Zerbi, obvious suspect –
He has declared he likes cucumbers
best.

ZERBI (*sings*). They framed him with
the theft of the cucumbers
And from then on they had his
number.
Not only did he get the sack
But they clapped a deportation order
on his back.
(*Spoken.*) But Zerbi was smart, Zerbi
shot through again
Before they could get him on board a
plane.

ALL IN CHORUS. The Zerbi hunt is
on!
Zerbi's a wanted man.
And he must flee and he must run
As fast and as far as he can.
They say Zerbi knows no fear
He leaves no trail behind him
And the Zerbi-hunters are scared to
death
Of what he'll do when they find him!

MOTHER. They're going to run Zerbi to
ground!
But maybe it's his lucky day
And he'll take the train to Marseilles.

JULIE. Or maybe he'll manage to start a
new life
With a nice suburban girl for his wife.

*Silence follows this child's voice full of
hope. A moment of emotional silence*

then thunderous applause, first from
GERMAIN, *then* LOUIS, *then the*
MOTHER, *then* ZERBI, *then the*
beaming JULIE.

GERMAIN. What about an encore, eh,
Mister Zerbi . . .

ZERBI. Certainly, my little blond-
headed one.

He carries on, the music starts up again.
He mimes out this tale of hide and seek.

I took to the hills, in the métro
When they're at Chatelet, I'm at
Trocadero
When they're at Trocadero,
I pop up at Porte Maillot.
And all this for a bloody crate!

I jump on the number 65 bus
And there I am at Porte Saint-Ouen
Just as they're coming up at Pantin!

ALL IN CHORUS. The hunt is on for
Zerbi!
Zerbi better take care!

ZERBI (*interrupting the chorus*). At
Saint-Ouen, and down in Marseilles
They're using guns these days.
Yesterday it was Laouri Mahammad, a
kid of seventeen.
The cop just fired straight at him –
The back seat is still covered in blood.
Listen to the wind of anger,
Listen to the mother's cries.
And that's how it was at Saint-Denis,
at Lille or Orléans,
And that's how it was in Marseilles.

ALL IN CHORUS. Ah yes, the Zerbis!
You better learn to take care!
All the Zerbis around that time
You better learn to take care!

ZERBI (*sings and plays with broom*).
One day there was a demo
Over near the Bastille
The cops lined up and charged the
crowd
And the marchers had to flee
Everyone bolted for the métro.

ALL IN CHORUS. Everyone was out
after Zerbi
Zerbi better learn to take care.

ZERBI. Another time in the métro
As I got to the barricade
The cops were checking people's
papers
It was a raid.

But I'd just bought myself a camera
A cheap one, at Quai de la Rapée,
And I mingled with the Japanese
tourists
And slipped through their net that day

Since then I never go out
Without my Nikon or Leica
And I look like any other tourist
From Russia or Canada or
Bandaranaika.
No more checks or expulsions or
arrests for Zerbi.

JULIE. Ah! All the Zerbis around that
time
Zerbis had to learn to take care.

During Zerbi's Complaint, the
MOTHER *has disentangled herself*
from the hose and has got herself back
into a decent state: hat, powder, rouge,
shoes, and GERMAIN *has tidied up*
the little house. The CHILDREN
applaud at the end of the song.

ZERBI (*spotting the cupboard*). But what
is in this locked cupboard?

CHILDREN. Nothing! Nothing!
Nothing to eat!
To suck or chew or wear on your feet!
No bread, no wheat,
No fruit, no meat.
It's empty, we repeat.

ZERBI *goes to the forbidden cupboard.*
Everyone holds their breath. He opens
the cupboard, and gives a big whistle of
admiration as he takes out a new suit on
a hanger.

ZERBI. Oh, what a lovely suit I've
found,
White, with stripes that go up and
down.

LOUIS. That's grandpa's suit from his
wedding day.
It's quite a while since he went away.
He went to the bookies to place a bet
And he must've won, 'cause he's not
back yet.

JULIE. You can keep it. *He* won't be
coming back.

GERMAIN. It's just your style.

Meanwhile the MOTHER *has turned*
on the radio. ZERBI *puts on the*
grandfather's striped suit. The
CHILDREN *hand him a snazzy pair of*
shoes that were lying about behind the

cupboard. He trims his moustache with the razor. The MOTHER *sends her little brood to bed.*

MOTHER. Go to bed, my little chickadees.
You should have been asleep long ago.
You've had a busy day.

The CHILDREN *run to the bed, rubbing their eyes. Over the radio is coming that slinky music that urges the body to dance, while the sandman of the blond desert of Araby passes back and forth like an angel over the bed. The* MOTHER *and* ZERBI *cast a tender glance at the little lambkins already snoring gently . . . and the tender glance becomes a tender, languid glance, and with this kind of music it's only one more step . . .*

ZERBI. They're sound asleep, the precious little insects.

MOTHER. The silvery sandman from the great desert of Araby must have passed like a winged angel above their bed.

The music is having more and more of an effect.

Like to dance?

ZERBI *is completely flabbergasted.*

ZERBI. Dance? Me? Would I like to –

Conversation as they dance.

MOTHER. You won't take advantage of the situation?
Because if you attack me without asking first
There's no one to witness my agitation
No one to save me from violation
And you can do your worst.

ZERBI. But what if Marcel comes back?

MOTHER. We'll just ask him to sit down quietly and count the money in the safe.
We'll say,
'It's the tango hour, Marcel,
The tango hour in the chic hotel.
You can pour us a glass of muscatel.
The children are sleeping, tucked up snug.
You can hardly blame us for cutting a rug.
"Play it again, Sam!"'

They dance more and more languidly.

MOTHER. I heard a story from the lady next door
About what happened to her sister-in-law.
She was caught in the métro between two stations
In a very awkward situation.
But now I've got used to the feeling
It's even rather appealing.

ZERBI. But the children might wake up.

MOTHER. They sleep so soundly, not even a cannon going off would wake them.

ZERBI. Is the bed any good?

MOTHER. It's nice and bouncy, and the springs don't squeak, and I air the blankets once a week. Yes it is good, very good indeed. And Marcel's miles away by now. I'm sure he's never coming back. Either he's still poking round in the swamp, or he's gone home to his mother. The safe was much too heavy. The great slob's probably let it slip back into the prickly rushes. And anyway, I might as well tell you, that big tub isn't the father of my children.

ZERBI. I thought as much . . . I got a distinct impression, as soon as I walked in.

MOTHER. So you see what I'm getting at? Circumstances being what they are, you can take advantage of the situation as much as you like. I won't even scream – except maybe just a tiny little bit, when I fall on the bed.

Just as they fall on the bed, someone knocks at the door. In fact for the last few moments two new characters have been coming out of the dream-like fog. They stamp their feet at the door in the snow and the freezing wind. The first one, very stylish, is dressed in wig and ribands like a king of France. The second, who has a hangdog look about him, is dressed in the manner of a muscly wet-nurse or poorhouse cook of the last century in a bluish dress, white apron and bonnet – a bit like a peasant in a painting by Breughel. The king is carrying a big bunch of wild flowers and a parcel from the neighbourhood bakery. The cook is pushing a trolley of an institutional sort, that is used in school canteens or lunchrooms. On its side is written 'Élysée-Montmartre school canteen'.

VOICE (*from outside the door*). Anyone home?

MOTHER. Good heavens! Not again!
Who can it be at this hour of night
Disturbing the sleepers all tucked up tight?
An innocent person could die of fright
With this banging and knocking in the freezing night.

Standing on the bed, the CHILDREN *launch into the warlike little counting rhyme, as if to psyche themselves up.*

CHILDREN. Axe! Drama! Crime!
Blood and guillotine!
Crash, bash, mash, slime!
Axe! Drama! Crime!

VOICE (*outside the door*). Is anyone home?

ZERBI. Fast, Germain, go and see who it is – but you just put one toe out of line, Little Germain, and I'll cut your brother's and your sister's and your father's and your mother's and your mother's cousin's throat, and I'll set fire to the house, and then I'll slit your throat as well. Get it?

GERMAIN. Got it, Uncle Zerbi Larbi! Message received and understood! Everyone here is on your side.

GERMAIN *looks through the keyhole, and does the trick with the sword again.* JULIE *and* LOUIS *squint over his shoulder. Outside the door the newcomers are starting to get impatient. Historical parenthesis: the* MOTHER *has also crept up on tiptoes and had a squint through the keyhole.*

MOTHER. Good grief! It's the king and queen!
Can it be? We've travelled back in time!

JULIE (*stunned*). What did you say, Mummy?

MOTHER. I said, it's the king and queen.

LOUIS. There is no king in France,
There's not even a king in England.
In England they've got a queen,
Or even two
If you count the other one too.

JULIE. Poor Little Louis, you don't understand, as usual. Mummy has already explained. This is just a story from the olden days, but a kind of *recent* olden days, see?

LOUIS. That's what I mean.
It's not the real olden days,
Not the olden days of yesterday.

GERMAIN. Inside my head everything keeps spinning and getting mixed up.
The past, the present, the future,
It's terribly hard to understand.

Outside, the others impatiently look for the bell.

KING. Come on, Gorillo, do something.
Stir yourself, ring the bell, ding the bell,
Wake up, Gorillo, wake up!

COOK (*examining the door frame*). Chief!
There isn't a bell!
All I can find is a keyhole there
Looking the worse for wear.

He looks through the keyhole through which Little Germain is jiggling the sword.

GERMAIN. I think it must be the Salvation Army
There's an arm out there as fat as a salami.

COOK. We've come for dinner. Open up. The noodles will get cold.

ZERBI. For dinner?
Little Germain,
Tell him there's nothing here to eat.
Tell him to try the next house in the street.
And if you put one toe out of line,
Little Germain, I'll slit your brother's and your sister's and your mother's and your mother's cousin's and your mother's father's cousin's throat, and I'll slit your throat too, Little Germain – understand?

GERMAIN. Roger, Uncle Zerbi.
Received and understood.
(*Speaking through the door.*) Mister Man, outside the door,
The cupboard's bare.
We're dying of hunger here.
We've got nothing at all to gnaw.
So be on your way.

JULIE. And our father always told us,

Since we were very small,
Never to open the door to strangers
Even if they cry and call –
Specially at night.

KING. But listen, dear child,
We are not strangers!
It's your king, the Lord's anointed
Open up! You won't be disappointed!
He's brought you something nice to eat –
Some meat, a sweet, a royal treat!

ZERBI. A king??
There's no king here
Nobody here is royal.
We're only an honest working family
Recovering from a day of weary toil.

KING. No, friend, 'tis your king of France!
He comes with his cook to dine with you
In all possible pomp.

LOUIS. There's no pomp here.
If your bike's got a flat tyre,
The cyclist can go to the garage down the road, or else the valet can go there on foot.

MOTHER. Right! We have to do something.
There's no escape: Destiny waits at the door.
(*To* ZERBI.) We'll make short work of these two.
You're my husband, OK? Marcel Zerbi!
And maybe by the end of it we'll get a meal for free.
Right! I'm going to open up.

They all rush to household occupations. ZERBI cuts wood, and the CHILDREN, brooms in hand, await the newcomers. The MOTHER, with a couple of well-aimed kicks, tidies up the things lying about, readjusts her hat and dress, and turns on the radio. A stormy wind is already blowing into the house. The KING, GORILLO alias Miss Marguerite and her steaming trolley enter sniffing.

KING. We have come for dinner.
The radio must have announced our arrival.

MOTHER. Ignore the mess.
We sort of forgot to make the beds.
Marcel, turn it down, for heaven's sake,
We can't hear ourselves think.

KING. Flowers of every hue for the lovely mother!
Cream cakes for the charming children!

(*To* GORILLO *who is having trouble getting in due to the mess and the fact that* GERMAIN *and* JULIE, *sniffing the trolley, are blocking his path.*)
Come in, come in!

GORILLO. Here I come, Chief, I'm coming, Chief.

LOUIS (*to the* KING). I hope there's some chocolate éclairs.

KING. ???

MOTHER (*taking the bouquet*). Oh, how sweet! Wildflowers!
Marcel, Marcel! Wild flowers!

(*To* LOUIS.) Say thank you to the gentleman, for the cakes.

LOUIS (*throwing his broom and snatching the parcel*). Are there any chocolate éclairs or aren't there?

MOTHER (*throwing bouquet at* MARCEL ZERBI). Marcel, Marcel!
Wild flowers! . . . Marcel, can't you turn it down?

JULIE (*echoing*). Marcel! Wild flowers!

ZERBI *sticks the flowers in the bucket under the table, then into the water jug.*

KING (*seeing* LOUIS *messing up the packet*). Don't open it – don't open it, I tell you!

LOUIS. Are there any chocolate éclairs or aren't there?

KING (*grabbing the parcel back and speaking more loudly*). There *aren't* any!

MOTHER. I'd like to present to you my little brood.
Oh, where have they got to now?
The eldest here – his education isn't lacking.
We've had the time to give him a decent whacking.

GERMAIN (*falling into the food trolley*). Mummy! Mummy! There's creamed brains in here!

GORILLO (*in one breath he lets fly his tirade, everything he's been keeping back since he first came in, meanwhile trying to fend off attacks on his trolley, and pulling out* GERMAIN *who's climbed right into it.* JULIE *jumps back quickly when kicked by* GORILLO). Come on now, dear, be good, go to your mother, you'll get some in a minute, yes, it's creamed brains, your mummy's calling you, are you bloody deaf or something, did you understand what I said, go to your little brother – get it, squirt? That's the rules, go to your mother!

MOTHER. Now settle down, and say hullo. You could at least have had a wash, really, look at these filthy disgusting ears, and what dirt have you been rubbing your noses in? Give the parcel back to the gentleman or he'll be angry. Say hullo or you'll get it! Say hullo!

LOUIS. Do I say hullo, or do I go and have a wash? Make up your mind, and anyway there's no soap left in the house.

MOTHER. Don't you dare answer back, and wipe your nose. (*To the* KING.) Really, it's too much, they always want to have the last word.

LOUIS. You don't have to yell, I'm standing right here.

MOTHER. Don't put your nose in your mouth and put your hand over it when you cough.

LOUIS. I didn't cough. It's the ghost of Ernest that's pushing me. In the night he takes all the blanket. Here, keep your bloody parcel if there's no éclairs in it. (*He throws it roughly at the* KING.)

MOTHER. Oh, you lout! Excuse him. You know how children are . . . and besides, the schools, these days . . .

LOUIS. These days?? There isn't school, it's the holidays. We can sit around twiddling our thumbs. Do you want to twiddle yours too, Mister?

GERMAIN *or* JULIE *has tipped headfirst into the food trolley.* GORILLO *tries to yank him/her out by the bum. He/she emerges all coated in flour, chocolate-eyed, metamorphosed.*

JULIE. Mummy! Mummy! Germain's

been taken ill!

GORILLO (*tea towel in hand*). Don't worry about it, madam, we'll clean him up, come here, darling, come here . . .

GERMAIN (*to* KING). So, you've come to fix the telly? Not a minute too soon – our thumbs are sore from being twiddled. (*Shouting the glad news to brother and sister.*) Little Louis, Julie, they're going to fix the telly.

KING (*preferring not to contradict him*). We'll have a go. We promise. We promise we'll try.

LOUIS. Trying's not good enough – you have to succeed!

KING (*taking advantage of a pause*). Miss Marguerite, come on, set the table. Don't dawdle! Don't mess about!

LOUIS. Yes! Don't dawdle! Don't mess about!

MOTHER. Children, help Miss Marguerite set the table.

GORILLO. No, thank you. Anything but that. Go and play, kids. Madam – let your little lambkins go and play.

MOTHER. Certainly not! They have to help. Don't stand on ceremony. They've been well trained, these little chickens.

No sooner said than done. In a trice the three urchins set the table instead of the cook who, supple and athletic, catches the plates which whirl low in the air like UFOs or frisbees, specially as the crockery and linen are kept in suitcases on top of the wardrobe. The kids set the table at a diabolical speed: in two shakes of a rat's tail it is set; the kids, knife and fork in fists, are sitting in front of their plates ready to attack the food. Everyone is sitting down. GORILLO *gets out of the trolley an enormous cauldron of spaghetti and puts it in the centre of the table. Then the tomato sauce, after dumping in the middle of the table several shoes – curiously reminiscent of those of the dead grandfather and dead Ernest. During this sinister whirlwind of a meal, the* MOTHER *presents* ZERBI LARBI *to the* KING.

MOTHER. My husband . . . Marcel, you could at least stand up, the guests have been here for quite some time.

KING. It's quite all right – he was absorbed in the news.

ZERBI (*with his huge broom behind his chair like a sceptre*). I've been working like a dog all day. It's hard to get up out of the chair, once I've sat down. (*Looks out from under his eyebrows as he untangles his spaghetti.*) They said over the radio that the missis was coming with you . . .

KING. She had the flu, and then her gammy leg started to play up, And then we got caught in a terrible storm – Luckily Miss Marguerite has a nose on her like a hunting dog, Haven't you, Miss Marguerite?

MISS MARGUERITE (*sniffing the air interestedly, and chasing flies away from the plates*). Yes, chief.

GERMAIN *is getting tangled up in some rubber bands mixed up with the spaghetti. Food projectiles are flying about.*

GERMAIN. Help, help, Mummy, I've got rubber bands in my spaghetti!

MOTHER. Louis! Did you do this to your brother?

LOUIS (*whose face is all rolled up in rubber bands so that he's starting to look like Frankenstein*). No Mummy! I swear! Scout's Honour! Cross my heart and hope to die! (*He crosses his fingers and spits in the KING's plate.*)

MOTHER (*to JULIE and GERMAIN who have gone berserk with catapults, taking it in turns with LITTLE LOUIS*). Julie! Stop making those pellets this instant! Don't play with bread! Bread is sacred. Think of the starving millions, all the little Chinese children who die of hunger every day.

LOUIS. That's not true! That's just propaganda!

MOTHER. Don't answer back. Go and get your fork. (*His fork has gone the way of the pellets and has stuck in one of GORILLO's padded épaulettes.*) Do you hear me? Leave your knife alone and put your hands on the table. Germain! Don't stick your fork down

your throat like that. You'll puncture your tonsils.

GERMAIN. Mummy, they're rubber bands! (*He pulls out of his mouth an interminable rubber band, at least five metres long.*)

JULIE (*admiringly*). Lucky there isn't a fish hook on the end!

Religious silence and then collective applause accompany GERMAIN's *skilful performance. Further mastication and vacuum-cleaner-suction of noodles ensue, while* MISS MARGUERITE *serves up an enormous cauldron containing diverse remains of a macabre meal: shoes, a hand, ears, etc.*

KING (*to the* MOTHER). So, madam, this is your own charming little brood?

LOUIS. What do you think? We didn't suck the neighbour's tits.

JULIE. Louis, let your mother speak.

LOUIS. I'm only trying to stop her giving dumb answers.

MOTHER. Louis, one more smart crack like that and I'll stick this knife in your back, right in front of everybody.

Shocked looks from all the children and from GORILLO, *in the face of the tranquil authority of this remark.*

KING (*to* GERMAIN). And how are you getting on at school?

GERMAIN. Better ask the headmaster. If you like, I'll ask him and tell you the answer next time I see you, or else I'll ring you up and let you know. Write your phone number on a bit of paper and leave it on the chest of drawers.

KING (*hastily seeking an easier interlocutor. To* JULIE). And can you do long division?

JULIE. Can you? (*To* LOUIS *who is still in mid-transformation with his rubber bands/Bandaids.*) What's black and white and red all over?

KING (*to the* MOTHER). And how do these little lambkins amuse themselves during the holidays?

LOUIS. We wait.

KING. You wait? What do you wait for?

GERMAIN. We just wait. You know?

That's all right, isn't it?

KING. Well, I suppose so. Some people don't even do that much. Well answered, son. (*To the* MOTHER.) He's a very bright lad, isn't he?

MISS MARGUERITE. He certainly is. He's the smartest one. I bet he can even count up to three on his fingers.

LOUIS (*sharp as a tack, to the cook*). This is my finger, This is my thumb And this little finger Goes right up your bum.

MOTHER. Louis! (*Gives him a whack.*) You asked for that!

LOUIS (*getting up, very very offended*). You bitch! In Russia parents who hit their children get sent to the Gulag.

The MOTHER *chases him with a fork.* LITTLE LOUIS *runs away, gets under the table, over it, under it, all over the place. Domestic whirlwind, and the wind outside rises again.* LOUIS *hides on top of the cupboard and pulls up the stepladder.*

MOTHER. Get down! Get down! Louis, come here! Come here! Marcel, do something for heaven's sake. Don't just sit there as if you'd swallowed a broom handle! (*Out of breath, she sits down.*) Oh! They'll be the death of me.

KING. Come on, Miss Marguerite – serve the leg of lamb!

JULIE. Yes, come on, Miss Marguerite, serve it up – we're waiting.

GORILLO's *turn to plunge into the food trolley. A couple of hobnailed boots land among the plates, old runners, ragpicker's clodhoppers, clapped out shoes, along with a bloody piece of goatskin. Sauce follows, ladled out.* LITTLE LOUIS *nips back to his place and the kids set about attacking the food.*

GERMAIN (*to the* KING). Did you kill the sheep yourself?

KING (*suspiciously*). No, little snowy. She did. (*Pointing to* GORILLO.)

JULIE. I thought so. She's got a real killer's face.

MOTHER (*very motherly, to her daughter*). Come, come, Julie.

Silence again. More chewing. The remains of the shoe leg of mutton go flying into the trolley. A household game of basketball: who'll score a goal? The kids gather round the KING.

LOUIS. Tell us about the job you've got. Do you have to get up at six on the dot?

GERMAIN. Did you have to do a technical or a commercial course to get this lackey's job?

JULIE. Do you make a lot of money? Do you get social security and medical insurance and paid holidays? Are you scared someone else is going to take your job and you'll end up unemployed, or on the dole, or having to sleep in the park? Or even kill yourself, like that bloke who got laid off in Orléans?

GERMAIN. Do you get much time to twiddle your thumbs?

JULIE. Did you get a grant or was your father rolling in dough? (*Pointing to* GORILLO (*who is scratching his feet*). Why is he standing about doing nothing? He could be fixing our telly.

KING. Yes, Marguerite, why don't you fix their telly. And dish them out a bit more rice pudding.

GERMAIN. Oh no, not that – I'll spew the whole lot up. I'm stuffed right up to here.

KING (*meanly*). It's all those cream cakes.

GERMAIN. No it's not, it's the spaghetti. (*He rummages among his tonsils with* LITTLE LOUIS's *fork.*)

GORILLO *attacks the telly. Spanner, toolkit, fiddling about with buttons and channels. The TV starts to work, giving out a weirdly warped mixture of cultural titbits. Then it settles on one particular programme, but for a change the soundtrack is spoken in Arabic.* ZERBI *suddenly emerges from the newspaper.*

KING. Marguerite! Turn it down, can't you.

LOUIS. Yes, and hitch up your undies. They're down round your ankles. (*He's twigged the transvestism of the character.*)

MOTHER. Louis! You rascal! If you don't stop it I promise you, boy, you're going to cop it! And the rest you'll get when they've gone away. You street urchin! Oh! I'm going to faint.

KING (*aside to* GORILLO). Where on earth have they got to? The press should have been here hours ago. They've missed a couple of really good shots.

GORILLO. The storm must be holding them up. (*Flips through his diary in which the various visits are noted.*) Either that or they got their wires crossed. They must have got it mixed up with next Sunday when we're supposed to visit the intellectuals.

KING. Ring 'em up, Gorillo. Ring 'em up, why don't you?

GORILLO *rings up, and the* KING *tries to kill time. Pause while people go on eating.*

KING (*to* GERMAIN). Well, my boy, and what are you going to do when you grow up?

GERMAIN. Who, me?

MOTHER. Say something, Germain!

LOUIS. He hasn't really made up his mind yet. Last year he wanted to be a butcher's boy, because he loves black pudding, but he gave up that idea after he had appendicitis – that had a big effect on him.

MOTHER. The year before that he wanted to be a policeman like his brother, and the year before that, a pilot. And now what do you want to be, my treasure? A plumber? A hairdresser?

GERMAIN (*very curious*). Maybe I'll be a priest, but I'm really still thinking about it. I haven't made up my mind.

LOUIS. A priest? That's not a job.

GERMAIN. It is so a job.

LOUIS. It is not, because you don't get paid.

GERMAIN. You do so get paid. People slip a few quid into the poor box.

LOUIS. If you don't get paid, it's not a

job. For example, you wouldn't call *walking* a job, now would you?

GERMAIN. You could so call walking a job!

LOUIS. Give me an example.

GERMAIN. Well, a man who delivers the mail on a bike, and his bike breaks down, and he keeps going on foot. He gets paid, doesn't he Mummy? (*The* MOTHER *vainly searches her head for an answer;* GERMAIN *keeps talking, to the* KING.) What about you? Do you get paid for going to eat at people's places?

KING (*to* LITTLE LOUIS). So, you want to be a policeman?

LOUIS. Yes, officer.

KING. That's a fine job.

LOUIS. I wouldn't know.

KING. What gave you the idea, then?

LOUIS. My grandpa always used to say, 'Being a policeman is the biggest skive of the lot!'

JULIE. And as his father was always telling him, 'Little Louis is the king of the skivers', he thought to himself, 'Little Louis, you'll be a policeman – your future's all mapped out.'

GERMAIN. If you go in a straight line, it's the shortest distance between two points.

LOUIS. Also I don't like having to stand up – and they're always sitting down, on motorbikes or playing cards in those big blue buses parked near the Bastille.

JULIE. He likes the Bastille. You can get hot chips there.

KING (*to* JULIE, *as the TV cameras still haven't arrived*). And what do *you* want to do when you grow up?

JULIE. Me? Oh . . . play skippy, or be a nurse, or an athlete, or a trapeze lady, or a dentist, or play the accordion.

KING. Now that would be nice. Do you play the accordion?

JULIE. No, but I saw this bloke on TV who sort of wiggled his fingers, he was wearing this V-neck jumper, and he managed all right. So anyway I said to myself, phew, *I* could do that, that'd be better than doing long division or housework.

KING. But that bloke could really play!

JULIE. I'm not so sure about that. My uncle, well he told me how you can pretend to play, and in the background they put on this record . . .

KING. A tape, and you mime to it.

JULIE. Yes, that's it. You're quick on the uptake. See, Little Louis, you can . . .

KING. Yes, but the man you saw really *was* playing the accordion.

JULIE. That's what *he* said, but *I* didn't see him.

KING. What does your uncle do for a living?

JULIE. He goes on strike.

General silence. The CHILDREN *quietly leave the table and go about their business.* ZERBI *has kept on eating throughout, with his nose in his plate as a way of keeping in the background.*

KING. Your husband enjoys his food.

MOTHER. He always goes on eating peacefully, no matter what else is going on around him. The doctor advised him to keep his mind on his food, and to chew it up really well. Because of his digestion, so he won't get an upset tummy.

KING (*to* ZERBI). And what line of business are you in?

ZERBI *is busy eating and doesn't reply.*

MOTHER. Marcel, the gentleman's talking to you, he's asking you what line of business you're in.

ZERBI. What line of business? What line of business? (*Seizes his immigrant's broom that's been standing behind him and hangs it down on the table under the* KING's *nose.*) Here's *my* line of business.
It's made of straw and the handle's wood.
It's good, and it sweeps like it should.

This could be the moment for the CHILDREN *to do a broom dance, in* hoods like witches, the intruder-expulsion sarabande.

ZERBI. I sweep, I sweep,
I sweep all day and at night I sleep
Sweep the water down the gutter
Sweep all day for my bread and butter
Sweep to the right for a screwed-up paper
Sweep to the left for a chewing-gum wrapper
Left and right and twirl it about
And turn it over so it won't wear out
Sweep to the left for an ice-lolly stick
Sweep to the right for an old toothpick
Round the corner for a gob of spit
And back again for the poodle's shit
I sweep from dawn till the afternoon
I sweep all day with my broom
And I sleep all night in my lonely room
I sweep up rubbish and put it in the bin
And that's the line of business I'm in.

The children applaud ZERBI *thunderously.* GORILLO *scratches his head. His nose must be telling him something he can't quite grasp. During the broom dance,* JULIE *has grabbed her 'father's' broom and started to go round the table.* LOUIS *follows her.* GERMAIN, *with the hood on, is playing blindman's buff.*

MOTHER. Julie, Julie, put your father's broom down! Germain! Sit down, sit down! We don't play with work tools.

LITTLE LOUIS *sets his sister's witch broom on fire and the whole lot ends up in the bucket of water.*

MOTHER. Ah! They'll be the death of me.

The KING, *having dodged the sweeping of* GERMAIN *and the other kids as they clean up the splashes and puddles, gives a final glance at the door.*

KING. Gorillo, let's get out of here. Too bad about the journalists. Did you take some photos?

GORILLO. Yes, chief. Two rolls. (*He pops off a few more with his flash, and packs up his plates.*)

JULIE. So we're going to see ourselves in the paper?

KING. Yes, my little treasure. Sitting sweetly smiling beside your lovely mother.

GERMAIN. Did you take a picture of our dad, too?

GORILLO. Indeed, we did, my boy. (*Scratching his beard and his shin.*) Your daddy is very, very photogenic. And I keep getting this feeling that I've seen him somewhere before . . .

LOUIS. You might have seen him in a bar, or on the street.

KING. Gorillo, you can pack up. I am, madam, and shall remain, your most obedient servant. And now, refreshed, we shall withdraw and leave you to continue in peace the cultivation and nurturing of all that is finest and most precious in family life.

The kids jostle GORILLO, each taking a corner of the tablecloth and pouring the whole lot into the trolley. In two ticks the table is cleared and GORILLO is seen to the door.

CHILDREN. Phew! They've gone!

But just as GORILLO and the KING bang the door behind them, the corpses of Ernest and Grandpa fall out of the cupboard. A fresh clap of thunder.

MOTHER. Grandfather!

CHILDREN. Ernest!

JULIE. We've found them!

ZERBI. What's all this?

LOUIS. It was a road accident.
The brakes failed and over they went.
Grandfather was driving the truck
And everything came unstuck.
We were just hiding them in here
When you came knocking at the door,
Before.

JULIE. We haven't had time to bury them.

ZERBI (*examining the bodies*). Oh! la la la la.
Oh! la la (*in Arabic.*)
Now I'm really in the stew.
What on earth am I going to do?
I saw the look on that big gorilla.
They're going to think I'm the killer.

Outside GORILLO is helping the KING to slip into his coat. He stops and, pointing to the door, speaks into the KING's ear.

GORILLO. Hang on a minute, chief. (*He rummages in his wallet and takes out some photos*). Yes, it's him all right. That suspicious looking chap who kept bending dangerously over his spaghetti, chief – I recognized him. He's no stranger. He's the famous Zerbi Larbi.

KING. Zerbi Larbi? You mean Zerbi Larbi of Barbary on the shores of Araby? Faithful Gorillo! Are you absolutely sure?

GORILLO. If it's not him, I'll eat my hat!

He pulls various papers out of his wallet, including a series of photos in a folder. He points to one in the middle. He compares it with ones he took during the meal with his Instamatic.

GORILLO. Here, look at this, chief.
A scar behind the ear
Gold teeth up here
Silver in the rear
A touch of the tar
A tattoo, a scar,
He's tall and thin, with a great big chin,
And when he walks, his toes point in.

KING. Cross-eyed, talks with a stutter,
A profile that'd cut through butter.
It's him all right.
Good work, Gorillo.
No one could have done it better.
You've got a nose like an Irish setter.
Get in touch with Dan the Punter
Detective Sprat and Inspector Rat
And Scarface Lionel the migrant hunter.
I'm in charge of operations, Gorillo.
And don't forget the customary warnings.
That's protocol
(*Rubbing his hands and jumping up and down.*)
Fire at will! Shoot! Bombard!
Forward!

In the house ZERBI and the CHILDREN are dragging the corpses. Ernest is already in the fridge.

ZERBI. They'll lumber *me* with the whole box and dice.
They spot an Arab and don't think twice.
Let's hurry up and get this lot on ice.

GORILLO *is all fitted out for the attack, in gas mask, CRS shield, riot shield, nightstick, grenades, machine-gun and so on. He knocks at the door.* ZERBI *and the* CHILDREN *are surprised in the middle of shifting the second body. The kids leap into bed and hide under the blankets.*

ZERBI. What is it this time?

JULIE (*sticking her head out*). Can't you people get off our backs?
We've just had dinner and we're trying to relax.
And if it's the Red Cross, we've already made a donation.

LOUIS. Leave us in peace. We're sound asleep.

GORILLO. Zerbi Larbi, we know you're in there.
You've done your dash
Your goose is cooked
We'll settle your hash
The jig is up
The chips are down
Come out!
We're taking you downtown
We've warned you
You've had it.
Come out or we'll shoot.

KING. Attack! Fire at will! Shoot!
Bomb them! Blast them!
Crush them! Crush them! Whamblast them!

ZERBI, *the* MOTHER *and the* CHILDREN *build a barricade out of furniture, the door, the crockery, the cupboard, the mess lying about, in spite of shots and explosions. They get behind it, prepared for trench warfare which might last for years. Pillows fly. Deathly silence after this last bombardment, then a burning broom comes flying out and lands in* GORILLO's *trolley. But* GORILLO *parries the hit with the water jug:* GORILLO *is always sporting, fast, well-organized on the psycho-motor function level.*

KING. Hold your fire! Hold your fire! Ultimatum!
Zerbi, you rat! There's still time!
Send out the women and children.
You needn't think we'll let you off.
We'll smoke you out until you cough.

Beware – we're vicious and we're tough,
We're not afraid to play it rough.

Silence. Waiting. In the entrenched camp, ZERBI, *the* MOTHER, *and the* CHILDREN *tiptoe about, getting the grandfather's corpse.*

GORILLO. What are they doing in there?
This silence is getting on my nerves.

KING. One last time, Zerbi.
Send out the women and children
We're going to set the house on fire.
You'll come out blackened in your night attire.
And all of Paris, the low and the high,
Will raise a hand to shield their eye
As the flames from Zerbi's hide out redden the sky!

ZERBI. Zerbi Larbi of Araby will never surrender. (*Throwing a shoe and the remains of packets of spaghetti.*) He'd rather die in battle. He'd rather slit the throats of the whole family – the children, the mother, the old grandpa in his pyjamas – and throw them out into the mud all dripping blood.

As good as his word, helped by the MOTHER *and* LITTLE LOUIS, *he throws the corpse of Ernest into the attackers' camp.*

And in case you think I don't mean it –
Here's one and I'm just beginning.
See if this little brat's still grinning.

Corpse lands in the other camp. Pause. Perplexity in the other camp.

KING (*to* GORILLO). What's this? Go and see. What's in that very suspicious-looking parcel?

GORILLO. But chief! It might be booby-trapped!
It might blow up in my face
Scatter my brains all over the place!

KING. That's an order. Take the bull by the horns!

GORILLO, *grumbling, goes to have a look, bent over and rushing the trolley/tank in front of him. Slips on a string of spaghetti, but nimbly recovers his balance.*

GORILLO. Chief! It's the body of a nipper

With his blood drained out and stiff as
a kipper.
This'll look bad on the TV screen.
We'd better keep our noses clean.
And bolt before we're seen.

KING. Absolutely not!
I don't give in to blackmail.
And I've had it up to here with
hostages.
Continue operations.
Shoot! Fire at will!

*Second round of firing. One-man-band
manages some feats of sound among the
smoke and the projectiles; the battle of
the pillows and bolsters.*

KING. What's delaying our air support?
We have to bomb them back to the
Stone Age!
Now's the time to strike, while they're
in disarray!
Blow them to smithereens! Zamblast
them!

*Silence again after the second round of
firing.*

ZERBI. Right – you asked for it. We'll
heave out the grandfather. One, two,
three! Forward, grandpa! Forward,
kids!

*The bloodless grandfather lands in the
other camp.*

KING. Hold your fire!
Gorillo, go and see what it is!
And don't drag your feet!

GORILLO (*negotiates a couple of danger
spots with his faithful trolley; turns the
corpse over*). It's the old bloke in his
pyjamas!
He's been killed!
This Zerbi is strong-willed.
Listen, chief, I'm getting flustered.
The press are coming and they can't be
trusted.
One look at the bodies and we'll be
busted.

*Hesitation by the KING who flattens the
plumes on his hat. Over the barricade
there appears a white flag that ZERBI
has made out of his singlet and the big
broom.*

KING (*grandiloquent*). Cease firing! The
enemy wants to parley!

GERMAIN *and/or* JULIE *advance
with the white flag, over the barricade.*

KING. What do you want, my little
treasure?
You may be small, but you're proud
and brave.
It's risky to wander about in no-man's
land.

GERMAIN *and/or* JULIE. I've come to
negotiate.
Mister Zerbi says to say that if you
don't let him go, he'll chop up all of us
and he won't even care.
He'll cut us all into little bits
And our toes and our teeth and our
fingertips
He'll send to the newspapers and radio
stations
So you'd better withdraw to a distant
location
Or you'll be responsible for our
extermination.
Mister President, and you too Mister
Gorillo – you'll be bathed in the blood
of innocent children . . .

GORILLO (*scanning the horizon
anxiously, glimpses a TV crew or a
running mob of journalists*). Chief!
Chief! The journalists will be here any
minute! We've got to get *out* of here!

KING (*showing off for the press*). Hold
your fire! We've got them pinned
down. But now they unsheath that
most immoral weapon, blackmail
involving tiny children. Let the snipers
perched on the rooftops and balancing
precariously on window ledges put
away their rifles with telescopic sights.
Let the helicopters, the jets and the
navy return to base. And let there be
no doubt about it – the equipment will
be used another day! Already a child
and an old grandfather in pyjamas have
perished in this battle. Let the Arab
out, and the mother, and the children.

GORILLO. You've had it now, chief!
Here comes the telly!

KING (*still grandiloquent*). And you, my
dear, tell this Zerbi that he's in the
clear as long as he lets you all go free.
We'll even give him a half-price railway
pass –
Second class.

(*The* CHILDREN *salute and turn to go
back*)

GORILLO (*to the kids as they leave*).
Where are *you* going? Stay here with

us.

GERMAIN *and* JULIE. We're going back to our brothers, our sisters, our mother and Zerbi – we're going back to them – it's our destiny!

KING. My dear Gorillo, it's all over. We can pack up. That's it for today.

They put away their things. A helicopter takes off into the clouds. ZERBI, the woman and LITTLE LOUIS emerge from the smoke after quickly regrouping with GERMAIN and JULIE who've returned from the delicate negotiations which it was their mission to accomplish. With suitcases and bags, they put their heads quietly out the door, sniffing the cool morning air. They signal to GERMAIN who's lagging behind – he glances back, signs perhaps of regret at leaving the home of their childhood? From the next valley we hear the sound of the train climbing the hill; it has already gone through the tunnel.

JULIE. Mummy, I can hear the lovely sound of the train whistle.

MOTHER. Yes, darling, it is a train whistle. It's 3.10. The Marseilles express is stopping.

They get in to the train, represented by the pile of beds that helped make up the barricade.

GERMAIN. Where are we going, Mummy?

MOTHER. We're going, my darling, to Marseilles.
Your aunt will give us a place to stay. It's far away.

JULIE. Would we be right in guessing Mummy, that you're going to start a new life?

MOTHER. I think perhaps you might, my dearest Julie!

As the train picks up speed, the CHILDREN sing.

Down in Marseilles
There's no winter and the sea is blue
Down in Marseilles
We'll have a puppy, maybe two
We'll call it Fido or Kiki
Or Foofoo or Fifi
In memory of Zerbi

and the streets of Paree
We'll stroll
Arm in arm along the shore
We'll wear
Our summer hats of straw
We can afford the fare
We like the breeze in our hair
Can you smell the air?
It's healthy down there
For Mummy and uncle
And Germain and Louis
And for Little Julie.

End of song. Miles pass. They look out the windows at the passing countryside. The train's rhythm rocks the tired children to sleep. They all drop off, heads resting on the edges of their suitcases. Suddenly GERMAIN wakes with a start.

JULIE. What's the matter?

GERMAIN. I had a dream . . .

JULIE. You were dreaming?

GERMAIN. Oh yes! I was dreaming . . . The train got to Marseilles . . . and those two blokes from just before were waiting for us. Zerbi got down on to the platform. He walked across the station, and then he walked across the street. And we kept on walking too, walking along and along and along on the platform . . .

JULIE. Then what?

LOUIS. Then what?

MOTHER. Then what?

GERMAIN. And then –

Sudden blackout. Gunshot in the darkness. In the sickly light and the smoke of the train, ZERBI is stretched out in a huge pool of blood, his suitcase open, his meagre belongings scattered round him . . . The MOTHER sits up terror-stricken, the CHILDREN around her. The KING and GORILLO are seen a bit further in the distance in the dream-like smoke.

GERMAIN. The biggest one, he said to me, 'My dear,
Don't worry, you'll get your chocolate éclairs'.
And I said to him, 'You can shove your chocolate éclairs!'
Ooh, one day, one day, when I'm a grown-up!

JULIE. Ooh yes – one day, when I'm a
grown-up!

LOUIS (*picking up a magazine that*
GERMAIN had been reading in the
train). Forget it!
You're mistaken!
It was only a dream!
That was just a story from the olden
days.
Things are different now.

GERMAIN. From the olden days? The
real olden days?

LOUIS. Well, not really olden days, but
very sort of *recent* olden days, see what
I mean?

JULIE. Just the same it's olden days, you
know for as long as it doesn't come
back in the present.

GERMAIN. Ah! Inside my head
everything keeps spinning away and
gets all mixed up . . .
the present
the past, the present, the future . . .
the before, the after, the now.